DPS 115

DPS 115

Pictorial Quilting

Also by Nina Holland:

Inkle Loom Weaving

Pictorial Quilting

Nina Holland

South Brunswick and New York: A. S. Barnes and Company

London: Thomas Yoseloff Ltd

A. S. Barnes and Co., Inc.
Cranbury, New Jersey 08512

Thomas Yoseloff Ltd
Magdalen House
136-148 Tooley Street
London SE1 2TT, England

Library of Congress Cataloging in Publication Data

Holland, Nina, 1934-
  Pictorial quilting.

  Bibliography: p.
  Includes index.
  1. Quilting. 2. Coverlets—United States. I. Title.
TT835.H55   746.9'7   76-50196
ISBN 0-498-01944-6

PRINTED IN THE UNITED STATES OF AMERICA

Contents

Acknowledgments

First I wish to thank Joyce Grover, who introduced me to quilting. A consummate craftsperson, she constantly had information that I needed at her finger tips. In addition, she was a leader for the *Clinton County, New York, Quilt* — the impetus for this book. I am also in debt to all the quilters who worked on that project. Their ingenuity, spontaneous design, and good craftsmanship were an unfailing inspiration.

Jane Golden, Director of Special Programs for the New York City Bicentennial Corporation, was of invaluable help in gathering information about quilts made under the New York City Bicentennial Quilt Program.

Most of all I thank the many instructors, leaders, and quilters who shared their experiences and photographs with me. To name everyone would take as many pages as the Manhattan phone directory, because as many as seventy-five people contributed to the success of some quilt projects. Nevertheless it is their contributions that are the real backbone of this book.

Introduction

"Wouldn't it be an appropriate way to show Clinton County's unique heritage?" Thus a group of women in upstate New York chose quiltmaking to illustrate life in their community. When they began their pictorial quilt in 1975, they didn't realize that many groups and individuals in the United States were also reviving this old art form and turning it into a contemporary folk art. Pictorial quilting, a grass-roots phenomenon, has spread like wildflowers, adding dots of unexpected color over the countryside.

This book illustrates several hundred pictorial quilts that have recently emerged all over the United States. All the quilts pictured were made between 1970 and 1975, unless otherwise noted. They suggest how skills and design can be adapted for personal self-expression. How to design a quilt, appliqué the top fabric, create or embellish shapes with embroidery, and sew together the top, stuffing material and the backing fabrics with quilting stitches, are explained in photographs and words.

The book also introduces less traditional craft techniques — cyanotype printing, silk screen, painting, and dyeing — employed to create pictures on fabric. These processes are simple enough to prove that one doesn't need talent or training to make a fine quilt, but rather patience and a willingness to try.

Americans from Colonial times to the present day have made quilts for both practical and expressive purposes. Here are some of the reasons.

Quilts give warmth. Like our forefathers, we enjoy snuggling under a quilt. Air pockets, packaged between the layers of cloth, insulate us from the cold.

Cloth is available and reusable. Now, like years ago, we can easily find quilting materials. We can piece scraps to make a large cloth. Because it was expensive and scarce, early Colonists did not want to waste fabric. One good way to recycle fabric is to create a new material from an old one. Today using scraps satisfies our need to budget and conserve resourses.

Quilting tools — scissors and thread — are accessible and easy to take from home to meetings. We don't need to spend a lot of money or permanently give up living space for our work.

Quilts are decorative. In Colonial times, beds were visible furnishings. In small houses, the mother and father frequently slept on the first floor, the children on the second. The bedcovering — usually in a prominent spot — was a good place to add individuality to the house. A quilt top became the focal point. We still delight in the festive patterns and colors a quilt adds to a room.

Quilts are a vehicle for self-expression. Should we choose a bright color or a muted one? Pick large or small scraps of cloth? Invent our own designs or copy those made by others? All these choices reflect individual personalities. A unique self-expression results, and gives the special satisfaction that creating brings. Like American quilters of the past, we can gain confidence in our ability to show life around us. We can enjoy the fulfillment of original production.

Quiltmaking well suits the American ethic to

justify play with work. In the past, isolated farm or frontier women got together to talk woman-talk. The quilting bee, like corn-husking and barn-raising, was a big social occasion. While the women talked, children played beneath the tentlike quilting frame, where they too enjoyed the affair. In the evening men often joined the group for supper, dancing, and games. Quilting still serves as an excuse for friends to get together. Bees are again the frequent pastimes of many groups.

Although we share many needs with quiltmakers of the past, this activity has not always been a popular pastime. It did play a vital part in American life from the days of the early settlers to the late 1800s. However, for the first half of the twentieth century, mass production and the easy-to-buy merchandise that resulted, slowed the hand-sewing of quilts to a near standstill. People became accustomed to buying ready-made goods and accepting the manufacturer's aesthetic choices.

What revived pictorial quilting as a popular craft? A "back to the good old days" revolution is greatly responsible. The many editions of the *Whole Earth Catalog,* the emergence of alternative life-styles, and periodicals like the *Mother Earth News* bear witness to this revolution.

Remember the good old days for the sake of a simple life, for the sake of ecology, for the sake of communal experience. By imitating life in the good old days we can learn to abandon machines, or at least become less dependent on them, we can conserve resources, we can humanize the production of both decorative and useful items.

Although life for the mainstream today changes little, the tastes and ideas reflected in this revolution have touched the American scene. Young and old now recognize a sense of values akin to those of the good old days. Quilting mirrors these values.

Warmth, availability of materials, simple tools, decorative self-expression, socializing and a reaction against industrialization, all have contributed to the renaissance of quiltmaking. However, there is a negative factor that we should examine.

Quilting has a long tradition, but art activity has not been part of life for most Americans. Visual self-expression for the layman is rare. There are art students and professional artists, but they are the specialists. Art takes a subordinate place in the life of most Americans. To illustrate the point, compare the place of music to that of art in a teenager's life. How many contemporary musicians can a high-school student name? Many. How many contemporary artists can he name? Few. Many a student learns to play a band instrument for his own pleasure. Few students try their hands at art for the fun of it. Artistic creativity is rarely encouraged.

Here is another example. The housewife has learned to rely on patterns for her dress-making and needlework. She creates, but with someone else's ideas. Kits and pattern books are available on every magazine stand, but it is uncommon for the individual to choose instead to "do her own thing."

In addition, careful work is not valued as much as speed of production. Besides sapping confidence to create, patterns and kits invite would-be craftsmen to compete with the machine, and complete a satisfactory piece in a very short time. She is urged to use heavy yarns and large needles that produce a quick design. Never mind the possible delicate, intricate work that only time and patience can produce. Mistakes can be covered by, "That makes it look handmade." Good craftsmanship is rarely encouraged and often ignored.

Therefore it is unusual for the untrained novice to use her own eyes and standards of craftsmanship to express her idea. She has learned to be afraid that, "It won't look real," "It won't be as pretty as a kit design," or "It takes too long to make."

The new interest in pictorial quilting is surprising because in spite of these attitudes, many who do take needle in hand create a vital, visual statement with inventiveness and technical care. That is why this book not only shows how to make pictorial quilts, but it also celebrates the many fine examples stitched by contemporary folk craftsmen, whose work serves as an inspiration to all.

Pictorial Quilting

1 Quiltmakers-Who Are They?

Quiltmakers vary more in shape, size, and group affiliation than do marchers in a Fourth of July parade. The following photographs of a doctor, a professional artist, girl scouts, and just friends working intently, should encourage anyone to join in the fun.

Men and Quilts

Men are sometimes the unsuspecting victims of quilting fever. A son in Brown County, Minnesota, lost the sleeves off of a new shirt that happened to be the right color for a rendition of the Indian Chief Sleepy Eyes' tent. Similarly, two thousand miles away, in Contoocook, New Hampshire, another boy gave up his shirt tail for the portrayal of the merry-go-round horses. A few miles away in Hopkinton Village, New Hampshire, a husband forfeited his tie when it was dissected for the owl in that town's quilt. As Joan Holmes of Contoocook put it, "Some of our friends were in danger of losing perfectly good clothing to our scissors."

But the role men play in quiltmaking is not always so unintentional. Several women tattle on husbands who had to contribute their two cents worth to their wives' projects. For instance, Eva Jane Wilson had to reshingle, piece by piece, "Howard's Sawmill" for the *Clinton County, New York, Quilt,* when her husband discovered she had placed them incorrectly. While in Maryland, a husband insisted on varifying the flight pattern before his wife could complete her square for the *Anne Arundel County Landmark Quilt.*

A contractor up in Rockport, Maine, corrected the pitch of a roof before he would approve of his wife's square. And among the Oberlin, Ohio, quilters, one spouse complains that she had to change the garb of General Shurtleff's statue to satisfy her husband, a Civil War buff.

However, several men deserve full credit for designing quilts. Stephen Blumrich of Oregon and Ed Larson of Missouri, both professional artists, design quilts for others to execute. Michael James composed the *Somerset, Massachusetts, Quilt,* which women of the town then made and quilted.

Moreover, special attention belongs to several men who stitched and quilted their own ideas. Jim Balmer, an industrial designer, made his debut into quilting society with the antique automobile he appliquéd and embroidered for the *Birmingham, Michigan, Quilt.* Bruce Butterfield, in Plattsburgh, New York, also a novice needleworker, portrayed the house he lives in. The piece shows ingenuity in detailing and a likeness as well. A. P. Stefferson of Preston, Connecticut, takes credit for the anvil square on that town's quilt. Dr. Brewster D. Martin of Chelsea, Vermont, designed and sewed his own squares, and according to the ladies of Lake Fairlee, "was most helpful in showing us how to quilt."

Both Rosey Grier, a well-known football player, and Arte Johnson, comedian, have described on television talk shows their love for needlework. Rosey stitched and embroidered football players for his square on the *Los Angeles Celebrity Quilt.* Arte's square, which he needlepointed, spells out

Women in New Ulm, Minnesota, work on the *Brown County Quilt.*

Contoocook Village, New Hampshire, Quilt. Joan Holmes, chairperson. 109" x 94".

Quilted bedspread. Batiked by Stephen Blumrich. Quilted by Teresa Blumrich. 80" x 60".

Clinton County, New York, Quilt — detail. Made by Bruce Butterfield.

the word "different." Each letter shows a different type face.

Having taken more than a token part in quilt-making, perhaps these liberated men will inspire more males to do the same.

Children to Great Grandmothers

Young people may start their interest in quilt-making by observing, as two youngsters from Napierville, Illinois, do, or by being the official stitch checker, as Paul Shipe at Plattsburgh Air Force Base does. Children in Mrs. Arlander's third- and fourth-grade classes in Lexington, Massachusetts, learned about quilting while drawing and coloring pictures about history with embroidery paints. To finish their quilt, they hand tied the top to the stuffing and backing materials.

The children of Watertown, Massachusetts, discovered another pictorial technique, crayoning with fabric crayons. A new product, these crayons, when adhered to cloth with a hot iron, give brilliant and permanent colors. The public libraries of Watertown sponsored this activity in which young people from four to fourteen years of age participated. After the crayoned drawings were transferred to the quilt top, the children hand-quilted it.

The New York City Bicentennial Urban Quilt Program sponsored many groups throughout that city. In one of these groups Rita Panfel, instructor of young people at Roy H. Mann Junior High School in Brooklyn, New York, came up with a good introduction to quilting techniques. Under her direction, each student cut a silhouette of his or her hand and, with embroidery stitches, appliquéd it to the quilt top. In the tradition of signature quilts, each student then stitched his or her name. The result, a bold pattern of hands, is colorful and personal.

Nancy Lopez encouraged Girl Scouts of the Council of Greater New York to picture views of New York City with appliqué and embroidery. The detail showing a view of Chinatown affirms the success of this project.

Children in the creative Craft Club, Ozone Park, Queens, created the ambitious portrayal of *Games Children Play,* under the direction of Eunice Samuels. A careful look at each square will bring back happy memories to all viewers. Dianne Crawford's square reminds us of the days when we searched for a piece of chalk or coal to draw hopscotch on the sidewalk.

The intricate sketching and embroidery of the

Lake Fairlee Pictorial Quilt in progress.

16

Preston, Connecticut, Quilt — detail.

Celebrity Quilt, Los Angeles, California. 10' x 9'. Owned by
the United California Bank.

Quilters in Naperville, Illinois.

Paul Shipe checking stitches on the *Officers' Wives Club Quilt,* Plattsburgh Air Force Base.

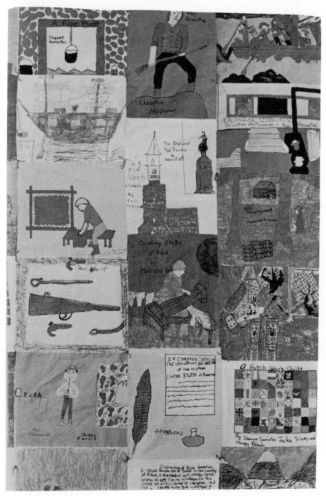

Historical Warmth — detail. Made by the third- and fourth-grade class of Mrs. Arlander at Harrison School, Lexington, Massachusetts.

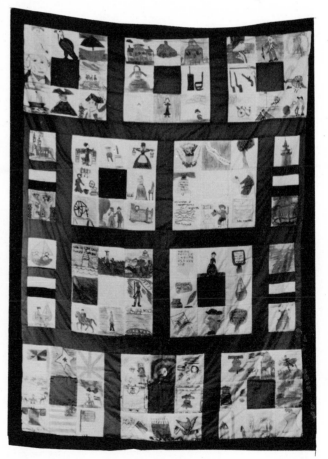

Quilt made by the children of Watertown, Massachusetts, under the direction of librarian Judy Burr at the combined Watertown Public Libraries. 98" x 74½".

Twelve-year-old Barbara Hawkes stitches on the *Watertown Quilt.*

Friendship Quilt, made in New York City Bicentennial Urban Quilt Program. Created by the children of Roy H. Mann Junior High School 78, Brooklyn. Instructor, Rita Panfel. *Courtesy Jack Lipkins, photographer.*

Girl Scouts View New York — detail, "Chinatown." Made in the New York City Bicentennial Urban Quilt Program. *Courtesy Jack Lipkins, photographer.*

Games Children Play. Made in the New York City Bicentennial Urban Quilt Program. Created by children in the Creative Craft Club, Ozone Park, Queens. Eunice Samuels, instructor. *Courtesy Jack Lipkins, photographer.*

Games Children Play – detail, "Hopscotch." *Courtesy Jack Lipkins, photographer.*

Lorraine Townsend with her "Empire State Building" patchwork piece for the *New York City Quilt*, made in the New York City Bicentennial Urban Quilt Program. *Courtesy Jack Lipkins, photographer.*

Worcester, Massachusetts, Quilt belies the ages of its makers. Seventh- and eighth-grade girls (ages twelve to fifteen) at Burncoat Street Junior High designed and executed this quilt, which won first prize at a statewide contest. With the help of Dolores Salvo, their teacher, the girls researched the subject matter and then drew out their ideas. After learning ten crewel stitches, they embroidered their quilt top. The girls describe how they solved problems that occurred during their endeavor.

When talking to the curator at the Worcester Historical Society, he definitely felt Daniel Gookin (first man to try to settle Worcester, but did not succeed because of hostile Indians) deserved a square. But all squares were assigned and only the two large center panels were left. "How can we do it?" we asked. "Have a man walking in the woods," was his reply.

One of the girls promptly drew a man on the large square of Worcester's Seven Hills confronting the Indians as Dan did, and we named him "Daniel Gookin."

We could not remember the color scheme of the entrance to the Worcester Public Library. When we called the librarian, she told us to be sure to use turquoise for the rug and orange for the chairs.

"We have gold crewel yarn. That should do, don't you think?" we answered.

Urban quilters putting the finishing touches on the *New York City Quilt. Courtesy Jack Lipkins, photographer.*

Worchester, Massachusetts, Quilt. Made by students at Burncoat Junior High. Dolores C. Salvo, instructor. 86" x 76". *Courtesy Marvin Richmond, photographer.*

Sun City, Arizona, quilters.

Schenectady, New York, 4-H quilters.

Montclair, New Jersey, Crafters Guild members at work.

Members of Continuing Education class, Fairfield, Connecticut.

Ozaukee County, Wisconsin, women proudly display their work. 84" x 70". *Courtesy James J. Schroeder, photographer.*

The Quilting Bee by Grandma Moses. *Courtesy Galerie St. Etienne.*

Tillamook, Oregon, Quilt. King size.

"No, that would not be authentic," was the reply. So off to buy some turquoise and orange yarn to be authentic!

Lorraine Townsend, age eight, holds up her "Empire State Building" patchwork piece that she adds to the *New York City Bicentennial Quilt.* Other members of the Urban Quilters who are working on this quilt illustrate that interest in quilting indeed bridges the generation gap.

The ages of the ladies of Sun City, Arizona, compared to the 4-Hers of Schenectady, New York, may be different, but the happy smiles and sunbonnets reflect a common enthusiasm.

Quilting Groups

Established organizations often form quilting groups. For instance, members of the Montclair Crafters Guild are pictured, putting the finishing touches on their quilt.

But other groups are specially formed so that people with this common interest can get together. New friendships are often as important a result as

Hudson River Quilt. Irene Preston Miller, organizer. 84" x 105".

the finished quilt. In Fairfield, Connecticut, the Continuing Education Department of the public schools sponsored one such group. A similar group was sponsored by the Newcomers Club in Theinsville, Wisconsin. About the new acquaintances it is said, "tongues worked as fast as fingers." Like the sewing bees of the good old days, a good time is a required ingredient of these meetings.

The Spread of Quilting Fever

Quilting fever is contagious. A typical smitten group is described by Audrey M. Peters of Tillamook County, Oregon.

I take all of the blame for the project, except for the small part that belongs to my husband. I had just seen the *Oregon quilt* for the first time and had been trying to impress him with its uniqueness, when finally I let him get a word or two in, and he suggested that I should make a *Tillamook County Quilt*. It sounded like a fine idea to me and we both gave it further thought. We came to the conclusion that a group could do a better job,

much faster than I could alone, so we organized the Tillamook County Quilters and at the first meeting tossed the idea into the members' collective lap. The energetic group started the quilt right away. Each woman chose her own subject for a block to create. The only stipulations made were that the materials be washable and the subjects pertinent to Tillamook County, like the cheese industry, which in fact was represented in three different squares.

Mrs. Peters mentioned that she was impressed by the *Oregon Quilt*. Members of that quilting group report that they had in turn caught on to the idea after viewing a picture of the *Hudson River Quilt*. This quilt, made in 1970 by women in Croton-on-Hudson, New York, was used to raise funds to clean up the Hudson River. It has inspired many individuals and groups. No grandmother can claim more handsome offspring than can this quilt. The chain reaction set off in Croton-on-Hudson reached to Tillamook, Oregon. This is just one example of the way pictorial quilting has spread.

2 Money-makers

Taking a cue from Rumpelstiltskin, that crafty dwarf with a spinning wheel, many groups have turned their threads to gold. Recently, quiltmaking has proved to be a good way to raise money. The raffling of a quilt has added dollars to projects all across the country. For example, the Old Campbell County Courthouse in Fairburn, Georgia — now a civic center — celebrated its centennial with funds raised by the raffle of a *Courthouse Quilt.* In the same way, the Ladies Benefit Society of Post Mills, Vermont, collected $3,000, at $1 per ticket, for their favorite charities. An added bonus for these women was the knowledge that the winner, now teaching quilting in Hawaii, will be reminded of good times in Vermont and in addition have a beautiful example to show her students. Likewise

In Fairburn, Georgia. Old Campbell Quilting Society working on *The Courthouse Quilt.* Double-bed size.

the band booster club of Portsmouth, Rhode Island, gathered $2,450, and the Alliance Unitarian Church, Montclair, New Jersey, $1,835.83 with their quilts.

Port Townsend, Washington, women have recently completed their fourth pictorial quilt. The latest one, *Trees,* a Kiwanis Club project, brought in $3,500, which was used toward beautification projects.

The Michigan Savings and Loan Association of Ann Arbor had another idea. They contributed a printed poster as well as the fabric to help the Calico Quilters make the *Michigan Heritage Quilt.* The poster aided in the project because people were encouraged to buy five or more raffle tickets and thereby earn a free poster describing the quilt. Over $3,000 was collected to benefit the Cobblestone Farm Museum. Of special interest is the signature of President Gerald Ford, a Michigan favorite son, in the quilt's center.

Rather than raffle their quilt, the Preston, Connecticut, quilters sold it by sealed bid. The money benefited their historical society.

Kay Luyden and Ed Koizumi designed the *Chicago Quilt.* Thirty residents came to their Contemporary Quilt shop to do the needlework. With a $10,000 minimum bid, they will auction their quilt and put the profit for the use of Hull House, a community service organization.

Bill Murphy, Administrator of the Siskin Rehabilitation Center Fund, describes how a quilt made in Chattanooga, Tennessee, gives them a continuing source of income.

Lake Fairlee, Vermont, Pictorial Quilt. 114" x 95".

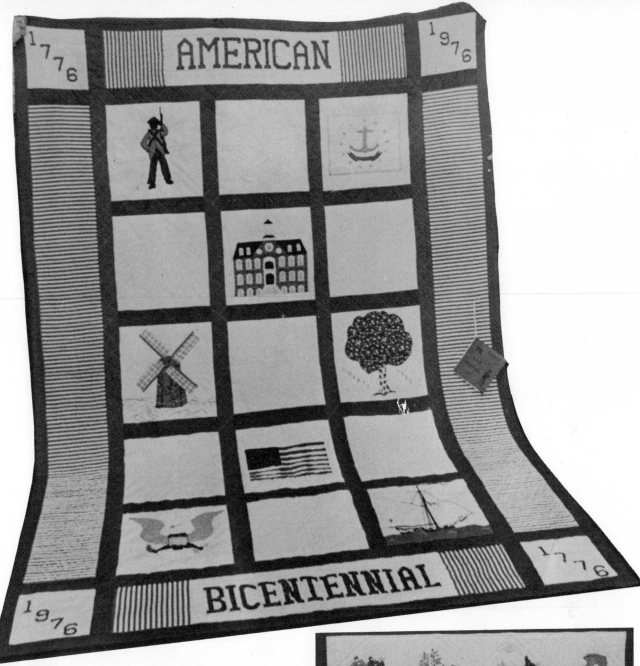

The American Bicentennial. Made by Portsmouth High
School Band Boosters Club, Rhode Island. Marie Thurston,
chairperson. 85" x 65".

The Alliance Unitarian Church Quilt, Montclair, New
Jersey. 96" x 76".

Michigan Heritage Quilt. Made by the Calico Quilters of
Ann Arbor, Michigan. Mayeve Tate and Pat Padala, leaders.
111" x 82".

Preston, Connecticut, Quilt. Made by the Preston Historical
Society, Inc. Corinna Brown, artist and coordinator. 86" x
61".

Chicago, Illinois, Quilt. Designed by Kay Luyden and Ed Koizumi. Quilted by city residents. 100" x 89".

Montclair, New Jersey, Quilt. Made by the Montclair
Crafters Guild. 108" x 96".

Map of the United States. Made by Tia Kolodzey. 72" x
120".

Somerset, Massachusetts, Commemorative Quilt. 101" x 98". Designed by Michael James.

From the *Lyme Town, New Hampshire, Quilt* – detail, "Fair." Made by Pamela Wilcox.

Chattanooga, Tennessee, Quilt. Made by the Chattanooga Quilters under the direction of Betty Breazeale. 12' x 10'.

Pictorial History of Pike's Peak Region — detail. Colorado Springs, Colorado. Made by the Silver Key Senior Services, Inc.

Trees of Port Townsend, Port Townsend, Washington. 104" x 90".

Mrs. Breazeale designed eight drawings, and wrote directions for them so that the needle-worker or craftsman may use them in many ways — embroidery, needlepoint, appliqué, quilting, etc. These additional designs are sold individually or in sets, and all moneys from them go to the Center.

The Silver Key, an organization whose major concern is the welfare of the low-income elderly, has the most financially ambitious plan for their quilt, which shows scenes of the Pike's Peak area in Colorado. The members of the Silver Key have solicited corporations to buy a square for $500.

When all thirty squares are sold ($15,000 worth) they will hang the quilt at the Pioneer Museum in Colorado Springs, and use the money for their charitable programs.

The Des Chutes Orthopedic Hospital Auxiliary is among the many groups who make money by quilting tops designed and put together by others. The Auxiliary charges $25 for a regular bed-size quilt. In December 1975, they turned over $1,050 (earnings of the previous six months) to the hospital. One of the tops they recently quilted was designed by Josephine Balcom (one of their members) and an art teacher friend. It shows many scenes of life around Yelm, Washington.

With these examples in mind, many groups certainly will not overlook money as a by-product of quiltmaking, when they plan future projects.

Yelm, Washington, Quilt. Made by Josephine Balcom. Quilted by the Des Chutes Orthopedic Auxiliary. 96" x 82".

3 Occasions and Themes

A theme or special occasion can inspire a quilt. The coffin quilt, a rather morbid example, was made in 1839 by Elizabeth Roseberry Mitchell. It pictures in cloth coffins with family names embroidered on them. As a family member died, his coffin was removed from the border and placed in the center graveyard.

Happily most needleworkers choose more positive subjects. Mrs. Lathouse's patriotic theme, *Victory,* stitched in 1945, is one example. Another more recent patriotic quilt depicts scenes from the history of the thirteen original Colonies. Sterns and Foster Company conducted a quilting contest in 1975. They combined the winning squares to make this quilt. Another type of national theme quilt that Sterns and Foster Company organized shows state flowers.

International symbols can also offer a variety of colorful images, as the quilt made by an in-service workshop in New York City shows.

Presents for children can stimulate many quilt-making ideas. Cherry Schwartz of Minnesota pictured nursery rhymes. "Little Miss Muffet" is a detail. The *Toys in America* quilt created by students of F. D. Roosevelt High School, in New York City, suggests another topic appropriate for a child's quilt.

Animals can suggest several different ideas for subject matter. The 4-Hers of Schenectady, New York, constructed a quilt that illustrates activities and interests of their club. Many domestic animals are included. In contrast, Susan Wallace of Bain-bridge Island, Washington, chose wild animals of Montana for her theme. The detail of the "Prong-horn Antelope" with its terry-cloth rump shows how a naturalistic rendering problem can be ingeniously solved.

Also an animal lover, Ellen Mueller picked ecology for her topic. Circuses, farms, and zoos all offer imaginative motifs for quiltmakers.

Clara Schmitt Rothmeier is a baseball fan. For her quilt she sent baseballs cut out of cloth to

The Graveyard Quilt (coffin quilt), Lewis County, Kentucky, 1839. 79" x 80". *Courtesy Kentucky Historical Society.*

Victory. Made by Mrs. Lathouse, 1945. *Courtesy America Hurrah Antiques, New York City.*

Thirteen Original States. Sponsored by Sterns and Foster Company.

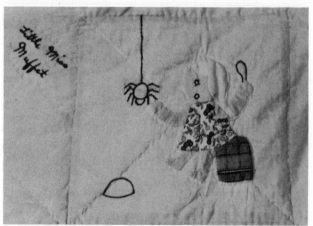

Nursery Rhymes — detail, "Little Miss Muffet." Made by Cherry Schwartz, Owatonna, Minnesota, 1966. 64" x 73".

Toys in America. Created by students of the F. D. Roosevelt High School, New York City. Maddie Appel, instructor. Made in the New York City Bicentennial Urban Quilt Program. *Courtesy Jack Lipkins, photographer.*

State Flower quilt. Sponsored by Sterns and Foster
Company.

International Quilt. Sponsored by the New York Board of
Education, Departments of Art and Home Economics.
Created by elementary school teachers in an in-service
workshop. Shirley Botsford, instructor. Made in the New
York City Bicentennial Urban Quilt Program. *Courtesy
Jack Lipkins, photographer.*

4-H project quilt. Owned by the Schenectady Museum,
New York. 104" x 93".

Montana Critters. Made by Susan Wallace, Bainbridge Island, Washington. 72" x 51". *Courtesy Nancy Tobie, photographer.*

Ecology — Idaho. Made by Ellen Mueller, Boise, Idaho. 72" x 66".

Signature quilt — detail. Made by Helen Thompkins, Washington.

Montana Critters — detail, "Pronghorn Antelope." Made by Susan Wallace. *Courtesy Nancy Tobie, photographer.*

Signature quilt — detail. Made by Helen Thompkins, Washington.

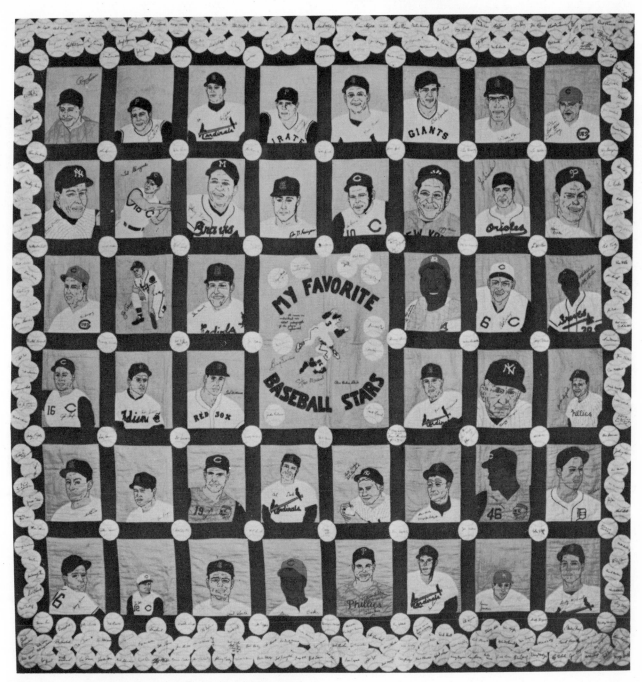

My Favorite Baseball Stars. Made by Clara Schmitt Rothmeier. 7' x 7'. *Courtesy Bourbon Beacon, photographer.*

Centennial Autograph Quilt – detail. Made for Louise Howe, Hadley, Massachusetts. Center, pen-and-ink drawing of the Agricultural Hall at the 1876 centennial exhibition in Philadelphia. Owned by the Schenectady Museum, New York.

professional players. They autographed and returned the balls to her. The many balls fly around the stitched portraits Mrs. Rothmeier copied and embroidered from bubble gum cards.

Signature quilts have a long tradition. The *Centennial Autograph Quilt* combines autographs with pictures from the 1876 era. A hundred years later, Helen Thompkins of Washington State combined bicentennial patterned fabric with the embroidered signatures of the ladies of her church parish. The quilt was then presented to the minister, and thus it reflected another custom, the presentation quilt.

Sometimes it is not a subject but an occasion that inspires quiltmaking. A tradition of friendship

Friendship Quilt, Baltimore, 1848. 100" x 99". *Courtesy St. Louis Art Museum, gift of Stratford Lee Morton.*

Bridal shower quilt – detail. Winona, Minnesota.

Bridal shower quilt – detail. Winona, Minnesota.

Friendship. Made by Friendship Quilt Group, Mountainside, New Jersey.

quilts (often referred to as album quilts) reached its peak in the 1840s. A popular quilt of this type was the wedding quilt. Friends of the newly engaged girl brought scraps and patterns to a quilting bee. There they competed to appliqué the most unusual block. Later the mother and the bride-to-be arranged and framed the blocks with other fabric. Friends returned to quilt.

Similarly, in the 1970s, the occasion of an engagement prompted Bonnie Schneider to send swatches of cotton fabric to all those who would attend a bridal shower for her daughter, Cherry. Contributions included a car pictured along a lonely road to remind Cherry of the first time she met her sister-in-law when she rescued Cherry and her fiancé, who had had car trouble; and two apples labeled "Apfel Kuchen" to remind Cherry that she had suggested that recipe (the only one that didn't sell) to her friend for a bake sale.

Friends of Gail Massey in Mountainside, New Jersey, have sewed several album quilts. Each woman chose the color and patterns of fabric she wanted for the quilt she would keep. She also designed a block. From each friend's bag of chosen fabrics, she sewed a copy of her design. At monthly meetings the women exchanged fabrics and completed blocks. The result was several quilts, each with the same block design, but each with a different color scheme — a color scheme to please each participant. Two photographs of the cat block show how different fabrics can change the appearance of one design.

The family of Mary Buffinton decided to create an occasion to express their appreciation of her love and attention. Of the specially made quilt Mrs. Buffinton comments, "I do think this is a delightful switch for the grandchildren to make a quilt for the grandmother."

Grandson, seven-year-old Colin drew a picture for his mother Katherine Campbell to stitch. Katherine also takes credit for the square that puts into words what the whole quilt expresses visually.

Mr. and Mrs. David Rankin also received an album quilt. Members of the Congregation of the First Unitarian Church in New Bedford, Massachusetts, gave them a presentation quilt that in turn inspired their new congregation of the First Unitarian Church in San Francisco to make another picture quilt to celebrate the church's 125th anniversary.

The retiring President of Middlebury College,

Friendship – detail, "Cat."

Friendship – detail, "Cat."

Mary E. Buffinton Quilt. Made by her family. 93" x 87".

Mary E. Buffinton Quilt – detail. Made from a drawing by seven-year-old Colin Campbell.

Mary E. Buffinton Quilt – detail. Made by Katherine Campbell.

Middlebury College Sewing Bee Quilt. Presented to retiring president and his wife, Dr. and Mrs. James Armstrong.

Presentation Quilt. Given to Mr. and Mrs. David Rankin by members of the First Unitarian Church, New Bedford, Massachusetts.

125th Anniversary Quilt. Made by members of the First Unitarian Church of San Francisco. 7' x 5'.

James Armstrong, and his wife, Carol, carried with them to their new home fond memories wrapped in a presentation quilt made by women on that campus.

The preceding examples of types of quilts illustrate only a few on the list of possibilities. Any event or idea can be excuse enough to start a quilt.

4 Layout and Design

Block Quilts

Appliquéd squares joined with a lattice of fabric are a popular way to construct a quilt. The *Back to the Roots* quilt, made by Michele Chisholm, tells a story, that can be read from left to right. She stitched each square individually because (as she found out) small lap work is less cumbersome than frame quilting. For this reason quilting in blocks is convenient for groups whose members carry their work from home to meetings.

On another block-style quilt, Eva Orsini — an ofttimes exhibited designer — worked with friends from the Unitarian Society of New Haven, Connecticut, in making a humorous and satirical homage to the 1976 bicentennial. Both the star and "vote" repeated patterns add to the quilt's visual continuity.

The creators of the *Onondaga County Quilt* devised a different system of block repeats. They used octagonals and the on-end squares that resulted from the arrangement. The organization had two advantages: it is a pleasant change from the more common square design, and like counterpoint, it offers two areas for embellishment.

However, the *Somerset, Massachusetts, Commemorative Quilt,* designed by Michael James, by creating a pattern of the windows, doors, and buildings, puts to advantage the quilt's rectangular shape. In fact the large shape of the quilt becomes subordinate to the small rectangles that fit it so well. This prize-winning quilt celebrates the archi-

Back to the Roots. **Made by Michele Chisholm, Unadilla, New York. 7' x 6'.**

tecture of Somerset and visually pleads for the conservation of its subjects.

Helen Bitar's works have been nationally reproduced and exhibited. In *View from My Window,*

Bicentennial Quilt. Made by Eva Orsini and members of the Unitarian Society of New Haven, Connecticut. 52" x 38".

Onondaga County, New York, Quilt — detail, "L.C. Smith & Bros. Typewriter." Made by Doris Holt.

Onondaga County, New York, Quilt — detail, "Wood Duck." Made by Sue Sherlock.

she utilizes the block motif as she repeats a vista of Mount Hood as it appears to her during the day and night, and through the many seasons. The harmonious colors vary in shades of blue and pink. The rhythm of the repeated triangular mountain shape fuses this sensitive composition.

The Old Campbell County Quilters in Fairburn, Georgia, alternated the repeat pattern of their courthouse with blocks of quilted white fabric. The arrangement is appropriately stately, rather than busy. The *Black Quilt* illustrates a similar device. The solid areas emphasize the pattern of repeated figures humorously bounding around the quilt's surface.

The scattered placement of different-sized rectangles produces a more informal layout in the *Me and New England* quilt designed and made by Pamela M. Senesac. The pop-art quality of the

Onondaga County, New York, Quilt. Mary Helen Foster, leader. 107½" x 90".

Somerset Commemorative Quilt, Somerset, Massachusetts.
Designed by Michael James. Made by Somerset Commemorative Quilt Group. 101" x 98".

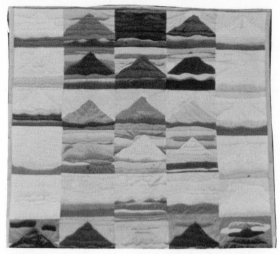

The Mountain from My Window. Made by Helen Bitar. 100" x 100".

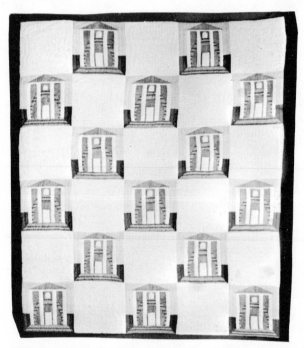

Old Campbell County Courthouse. Made by the Old Campbell County Quilting Society. 68" x 68".

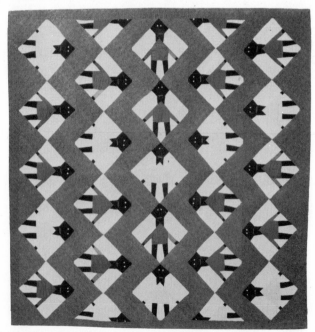

Black Quilt. Made in Southern Missouri about 1900. *Courtesy America Hurrah Antiques, New York City.*

Me and New England. Made by Pamela M. Senesac, Hyde Park, Massachusetts. 69" x 43".

New York City Bicentennial Quilt. Sponsored by the School Art League and Lower East Harlem Community Quilters. Created by students, teachers, and senior citizens. Margit Echols, instructor. Made in the New York City Bicentennial Urban Quilt Program. *Courtesy Jack Lipkins, photographer.*

Madison, Connecticut, Quilt. Mary Alice Bohn, leader. Owned by the Madison Historical Society. 90" x 86".

Crazy Quilt. Made by Rachel Jackson Lawrence, granddaughter of Andrew Jackson about 1848. *Courtesy Ladies Hermitage Association, Hermitage, Tennessee.*

Farrago. Made by Clara Wainwright, Arlington, Massachusetts. 60" x 47½".

Oberlin, Ohio, Quilt — detail, "Aerial Landscape." Made by Ricky Clark. *Courtesy Jean Tufts, photographer.*

contemporary signs makes this an accurate comment on life in the seventies.

The *Madison, Connecticut, Heritage Quilt* treats a historical theme with the same technique.

Crazy Quilts

The *New York City Bicentennial Quilt* previously shown under construction has a jigsaw-puzzle composition. The busy cloth patterns, jumble of cut shapes, images of traffic jams and city bustle, splendidly express the urban theme. This pieced work reminds one of the crazy quilts so popular in the late 1800s. These showpieces were status symbols that proved that a nimble-fingered woman had the leisure to do elegant rather than necessary work. Precious bits of velvet, satin, and hat trims were favorite materials.

Clara Wainwright, a professional artist, adopted this tradition when she pieced an autobiographical quilt she calls *Farrago*. Snips and scraps from other quilts she made form a kaleidoscope of color and memory pictures.

In a similar way, aerial landscape blocks from both Ohio and Kansas quilts reflect the influence of the crazy quilt.

Framed Designs

When a central picture is framed by border designs, it relates well to the quilt's basic rectangular shape. A classic example was made by Sarah Furman Warner, in Greenfield Hill, Connecticut, around 1800. In the same tradition, Hannah Stockton in about 1830 appliquéd and embroidered land and water scenes around a stylized tree. A more subdued example, entitled *Anne Hathaway's Cottage*, dates from about 1920.

Contemporary illustrations also show a central point of interest. A church, the focal point of the *La Grange, Ohio, Quilt*, is very reminiscent of the one pictured in the *Sarah Furman Warner Quilt*.

Another example comes from Vermont, where women chose a map of their state for the center theme. Pictorial blocks border the map with its embroidered details. Correspondingly, illustrations on the *Nautical Quilt*, sponsored by the Seaman's

Douglas County, Kansas, Quilt – detail, "Eudora Flats." **Made by Betty Hagerman.**

Sarah Furman Warner Bed Cover, **about 1800.** *Courtesy Collections of Greenfield Village and the Henry Ford Museum, Dearborn, Michigan.*

53

Hannah Stockton Quilt, about 1830. *Courtesy New York State Historical Association, Cooperstown, New York.*

Anne Hathaway's Cottage, Northern Ohio, about 1920. 93" x 77". *Courtesy the collection of Lynne Berger.*

Centennial, La Grange, Ohio. Jean Weese, leader. 110" x 94".

Church Institute in Manhattan, frame a large piece of moiré taffeta — a likeness of shimmering water.

The women of Douglas County, Kansas, centered their quilt around a barn, a country school, and cattle, things commonly found in the landscape of their state. Moreover, they employed another design technique. To further unify their quilt, they coordinated patterns and colors. A small, green print appears on the vines and leaves of the sunflowers, and on a detail of each square. The quilters cut all flags from the same fabric. The brown material framing each square covers roofs and tree trunks. Even the embroidered titles (not apparent in the photograph) were stitched in the same light brown — a color chosen so it would not detract from the pictures.

Stylized shapes on the *Dream Tree* quilt, made by Teresa Barkley, flank the central subject. When in her teens, Teresa made this quilt for her friend, Diane Smits, who loved to read and daydream in this tree.

Women from Plattsburgh, New York, Air Force Base worked out another axial arrangement. Buildings and symbols of military life radiate in a sunburst composition.

Portrayals of life in Pecos, New Mexico, swirl like spokes of a wheel in yet another example. *Combian Los Tiempos y Nosotros con Ellos* is one of the many quilts developed as a result of embroidery classes recently conducted in many New Mexico villages.

Single-Image Quilts

A single idea can be subject enough for a quilt. The idea for *Watchtower* grew, as Molly Upton pieced various sizes and shapes of black and white rectangles together. The configuration suggested ruins and then structures as she worked. *Watchtower* resulted.

Tia Kolodzey also pieced rather than appliquéd much of her quilt. As a child she spent many wakeful hours memorizing patterns and colors on her bed cover, instead of taking her nap. Now a mother, she decided that as her children wait for sleep, they can learn some geography. The result is this nap map. The shapes of many states contain traditional patchwork patterns. She was not afraid to let the map overlap the edge of the quilt's border. The arrangement adds to the casual and fun character of the bed cover.

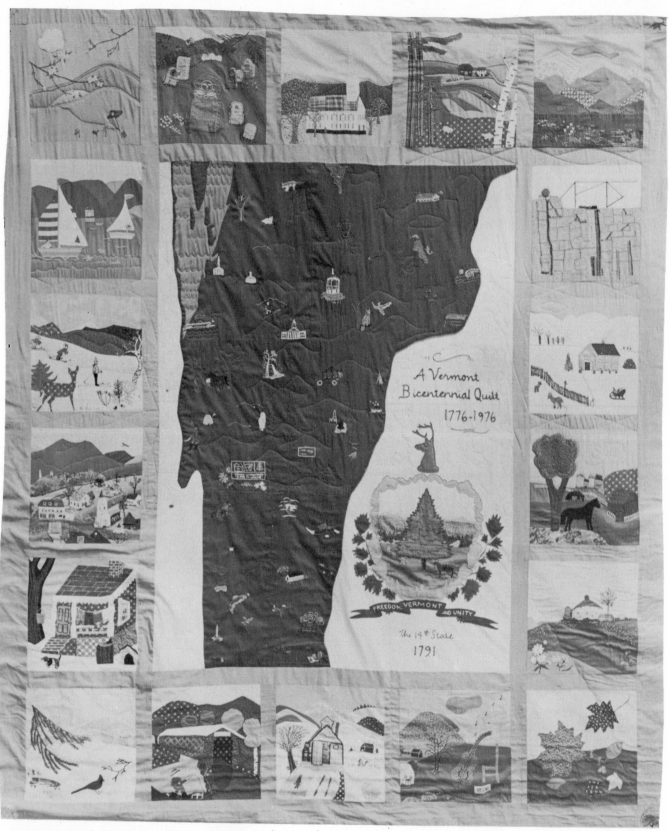

Vermont Quilt. Connie Cummings, leader. 112" x 96".
Courtesy Ellen Foscue-Johnson, photographer.

Combian los Tiempos y Nosotros con Ellos (Times Change and We with Them). Made by women of Pecos, New Mexico. Carmen Orrego-Salos, instructor. Helen Thompson, coordinator. 108" x 90".

Nautical Quilt. Sponsored by the Seamen's Church Institute, Manhattan. Created by community members. Celine Mahler and Anita Schlachter, instructors. *Courtesy Jack Lipkins, photographer.*

The Dream Tree — detail. Made by Teresa Barkley, Wilmington, Delaware.

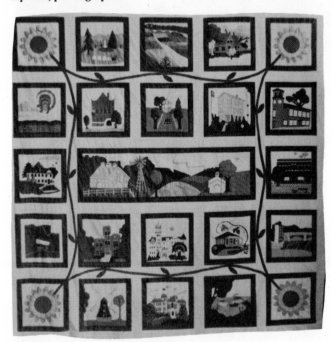

Douglas County, Kansas, Quilt. Louise Townsend, coordinator. 97" x 97".

57 *Plattsburgh Officers' Wives Club Quilt.* Paula Twells, chairperson. 73" x 60".

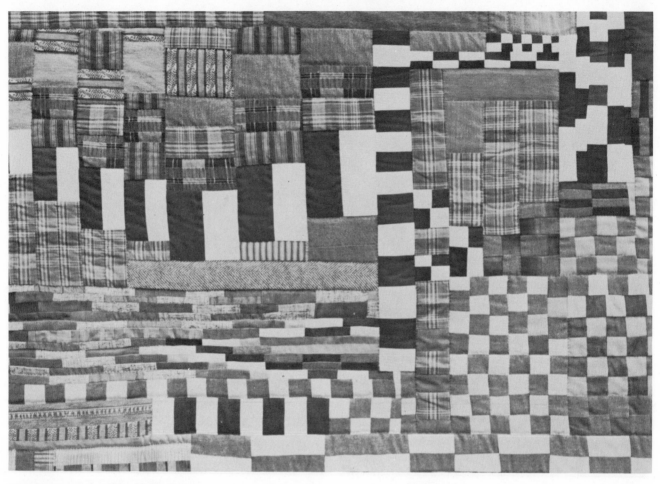

Watchtower – detail by Molly Upton.

United States Quilt. **Made by Patricia Quinan, Newton Hills, Massachusetts.**

Patricia Quinan's quilt shows another approach to the same subject matter. She has added seals, symbols, and profiles of presidents to her piece.

Susan Hoffman, a professional artist, calls her work quilted tapestry. The subject of this quilt, *Spires of Constances Cathedral,* is a Norman Gothic church built in the early thirteenth century. It reflects her interest in medieval architecture and life. In the previous examples, subjects were placed in a vertical-horizontal arrangement or around a central area. In Susan Hoffman's quilt, the cathedral spires soar in diagonal lines. The heaven-bound movement and the worm's-eye perspective emphasize the height of the roof peaks and the spirit of the architecture.

A foreshortened view accentuates the illusion of space in Michele Chisholm's *The One with the Swing* quilt. She uses another compositional device — framing the scene with the trees and foreground, for a three-dimensional effect.

Dawn Moser, also a professional artist, designed a quilt for her son when he was nine and loved

Map of the United States. Made by Tia Kolodzey, California. 72" x 120".

Watchtower. Made by Molly Upton, Darien, Connecticut. 90" x 110½".

The One with the Swing. Made by Michele Chisholm, Unadilla, New York. 7' x 6'.

Spires Coutances Cathedral. Made by Susan Hoffman, Darien, Connecticut. 76" x 72".

Erich's House. Made by Dawn Moser, Berkeley, California. 88" x 70". *Courtesy Ed Kirwan Graphic Arts, photographer.*

34 Station. Made by Carol Hearty, Brookline, Massachusetts. 96" x 81".

Birds in a Cage. Made by Mary Dunn, Ashland, Nebraska. 51" x 31".

34 Station — reverse side. Made by Carol Hearty, Brookline, Massachusetts. 96" x 81".

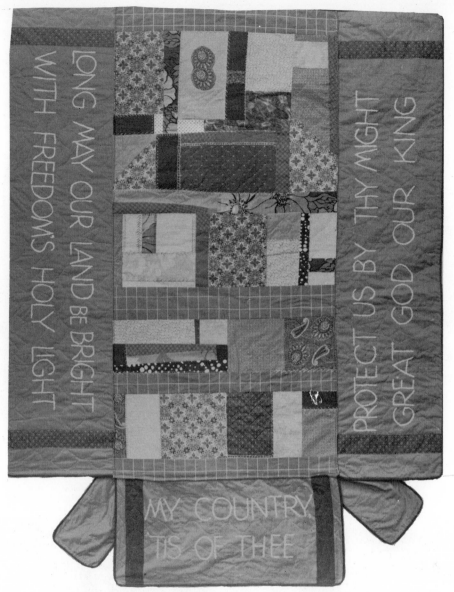

Quilted bedspread. Made by Sister Helena Steffens-meier, Milwaukee, Wisconsin. 104" x 80". *Courtesy Larry Krelewski, photographer.*

Pancakes, Butter, and Syrup. Made by Ros Cross, Los Angeles, California. 110" x 96".

Hopkinton, New Hampshire, Quilt — detail, "Town Hall". Made by Nancy Bemis.

Clinton County, New York, Quilt — detail, "Dannemora Prison Wall." Made by Jean Mullady.

Douglas County, Kansas, Quilt — detail, "Old Fraser Hall." Made by Ida R. Smith.

Around Puget Sound — detail, "Coastal Scene Near Cape Alava, Washington." Made by Betty Orians. *Courtesy Cathi Gunderson, photographer.*

to imagine a perfect house with a tower room for himself. *The Dream House* appropriately floats across her quilt.

Placement can connote a subject's stability or movement. It can also confine images, as this *Birds in a Cage* quilt, made by Mary Dunn, well illustrates.

For some artists, the edges of a quilt are no limit. Carol Hearty circumvented her quilt's edge and planned a second design for the reverse side. As her piece is rotated, the moon changes its phase and relates the two sides. The colors, shapes, and expressed stillness, repeated on the front and back of *34 Station,* further unify the entire piece.

La Grange, Ohio, Quilt — detail, "First La Grange Band."

The quilt of Sister Helena Steffens-meier, a well-known Wisconsin artist, goes beyond the usual rectangular shape. Like many in Colonial times, this quilt is cut to fit the top, sides, and end of the bed. The small pieces cover the bed's corners.

Bed covers of the professional designer Ros Cross often spill onto the floor in a cartoonlike representation of food. *Pancakes, Butter, and Syrup* is additionally displayed with a free splash of quilted syrup and a needlepoint bacon-strip rug — other creations of Ros Cross.

There are only suggestions, no rules about how to lay out a pictorial quilt, but as these photographs show, the possibilities are endless.

Designing Individual Blocks

A block should characterize not only the realistic appearance, but also a basic feeling about its subject. A happy memory, like the one of this horse and buggy, demands bright colors, and busy prints. By contrast, the penetentiary wall solicits a stark and severe treatment. The plain stone wall, sewn from a prisoner's shirt, is an excellent solution.

Here are some other examples. The skipping clouds and blooming trees soften the stately architectural lines of "Old Fraser Hall," on the Kansas University campus block. In this depiction, the viewer senses more about happy student life than about the world of academic studies.

The birds give a movement that mirrors peacefully lapping waves, in this *Puget Sound* landscape. The small silhouettes remind us that the scene is not static, and breathes life.

In the "First La Grange Band" square, the puckers of the quilting march right through the street, as if repeating the band's *ra ta ta tah* and *to to to to toot*.

There is no way to measure how much these design choices were consciously made. However, visual elements can help tell a story and add expression. By recognizing this, a designer can communicate his feelings.

5 Appliqué

The *Stewartstown, Pennsylvania. Quilt* displays a good comparison between the technique of appliqué and that of piecing. The geometric patterns, familiar to all quilt enthusiasts, grow from the joining of one fabric scrap to another. Many small triangles or rectangles are pieced together to form one unit. In contrast, the pictorial squares develop from layers of cloth sewn one on top of another — a method called appliqué.

A Brief History

Some of America's first quilters, in order to extend the use of expensive imported fabrics, cut a picture of a bird or a flower from printed cloth and stitched it to a background. In this way they decorated a large piece of fabric with a small, more elegant one. They then often embellished the appliquéd design with embroidery.

By the mid-nineteenth century, quilters had turned to their own stylized appliquéd flowers, leaves, and subjects from nature. In the late 1800s appliquérs treated more individual themes, which required the needleworker to pictorially illustrate her idea. It is this tradition that the quiltmakers of the 1970s have followed.

Hints on Illustrating Ideas

For those who want to try pictorial quilting, drawing is perhaps the hardest hurdle to jump. Some people rely on an experienced friend to sketch out the plan. But some of the most charming illustrations are made by novices who are making fabric pictures for the first time.

If you have had little experience in drawing, but are willing to try, consider some of the following suggestions. Look for pictures in magazines and books that you can use as a guide. Simplify the shapes and copy freehand difficult subjects like a bicycle or a dog. Or take some photographs of problem subjects. If you want to include people, have someone pose for you for a few minutes. Cartoons are also helpful guides for drawing simple figures. If a leg seems too long or a nose too short, ask a friend for an opinion, and then change it. Because cutout shapes are not detailed, your drawing talents won't be severely taxed. You probably will be surprised to find that indeed you can portray a house, a tree, and a neighbor.

How to Plan an Appliqué

The following photographs will show you step by step one way to plan an appliqué. For this quilt jigsaw puzzle shapes fit into a basic rectangle for the finished piece. Materials needed:

    carbon paper
    felt-tip marker
    needle
    pins
    scissors
    scraps of cloth and background material
    stiff paper
    thread

Kenzo's Super Heroes. Made by Michiko Sato. 7' x 6'.

Clinton County, New York, Quilt — detail, "The Battle of Plattsburgh." Made by Elaine Yingling.

New York City Quilt. Made in the New York City Bicentennial Urban Quilt Program. Instructor, Margit Echols. *Courtesy Jack Lipkins, photographer.*

From the *Brown County, Minnesota, Quilt* — detail, "Schell Home, New Elm, Minnesota."

Stewartstown, Pennsylvania, Quilt — top half. Jenni Sipe, designer. *Courtesy Stewartstown Public Library.*

Stewartstown, Pennsylvania, Quilt — bottom half. Jenni Sipe, designer. *Courtesy Stewartstown Public Library.*

Bedspread, 1782. 94" x 90". *Courtesy The Henry Francis du Pont Winterthur Museum.*

Friendship Quilt. Signed and dated "Aunt Eliza Moore, Trenton, N.J., March 4th, 1843." 101" x 104". 3¾" fringe on three sides. *Courtesy Daughters of the American Revolution Museum. Gift of Mrs. C. Edward Murray.*

Quilt — detail, appliqué, floral bridal, c. 1850. *Courtesy Daughters of the American Revolution Museum. Gift of Miss D. Loraine Yerkes.*

Pictures in Patchworks — detail, "Gossips," c. 1890-1910. Designed by Eunice W. Cook, Vermont. Index of American Design. *Courtesy National Gallery of Art, Washington, D.C.*

The Buffalo Bill Quilt — detail. Pennsylvania, c. 1880. *Courtesy The Greenfield Village and Henry Ford Museum.*

Make a scale drawing. As previously suggested you can use illustrations to help you figure out how things look. Keep all shapes simple. Divide your plan into workable sections. About twenty inches should be the maximum dimension. Outline the sections with a thick, felt-tip marker.

Draw two dotted lines, one vertically, one horizontally, halfway through one section. Enlarge the section to the finished size. The dotted lines will help you place your figures. In this example eight inches· at the top enlarges to sixteen inches in the finished design, so all measurements are doubled.

With carbon paper, trace a copy of your full-sized plan to a large, stiff piece of paper. Leftover wallpaper offers a good surface. Mark areas on both copies of your plan with corresponding numbers. Cut out the large shapes from one drawing. The cutouts will be your patterns for the color areas. Details can be added later. The flesh tone of shape No. 5 will repeat for the arms, legs, and head. So in a case like this, cut out the whole figure, not each piece separately.

Pin the patterns to appropriate colored fabrics. When you cut each piece out, add a quarter inch margin for the hem. On the background fabric, leave a half inch hem margin.

After the pieces are cut, unpin the pattern and pin the fabrics to the background by following your original sketch plan. Clip all curved areas an eighth inch. This will help you tuck the hem under smoothly. When folding the hems under, a seam ripper can help to poke small corners of material into place.

If your design has too many corners and turns to hem them neatly, you may want to try a machine zigzag stitch, which will cover the edge of your appliqué and keep it from unraveling.

However, in most cases you will want to use a simple running stitch or a hidden stitch to hand-appliqué your pieces into place. To make a hidden stitch follow these directions. Bring the thread up from the underside through the backing and the very edge of the turned-in hem of your appliqué. Now push the needle into the background cloth, right next to the point it just penetrated. Take a small stitch that will go through the background fabric and the turned-in hem of the appliqué. Repeat.

To add small details, use some embroidery stitches (shown in the next chapter). In this

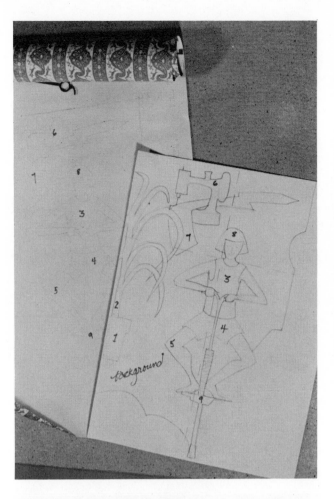

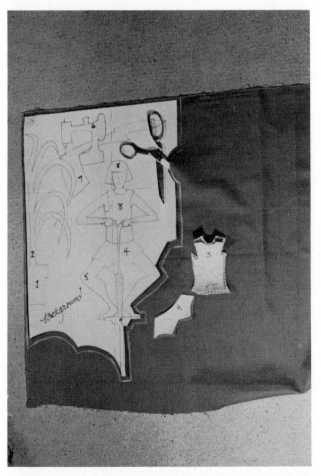

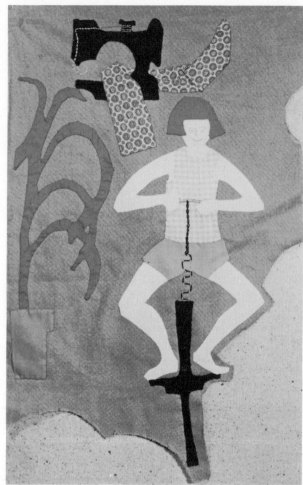

Gorham, Maine, Quilt — detail (machine appliqué). "Profile of Mary Phinney." Made by Mrs. Richard Borden.

Clinton County, New York, Quilt — detail, "Cumberland Head Lighthouse." Made by Ruth Blakeslee and Alice Sanger.

New York, New York: Still a Wonderful Town — detail, "Keystone Cops." Made by Minna Charles. Made in the New York City Bicentennial Urban Quilt Program. *Courtesy Jack Lipkins, photographer.*

Clinton County, New York, Quilt — detail, "Plattsburgh Public Library." Made by Sylvia Ransom and Joyce Martina.

Clinton County, New York, Quilt — detail, "Ice Fisherman." Made by Joyce and Michaele Martina.

72

Star quilt — detail, "Statue of Liberty" instructor, Shirley Botsford. Made in the New York City Bicentennial Urban Quilt Program. *Courtesy Jack Lipkins, photographer.*

Clinton County, New York, Quilt — detail, "Redford Glass Factory." Made by Vera Hirsh.

Clinton County, New York, Quilt — detail, "Skier." Made by Judy Corigliano and Anne Bailey.

Clinton County, New York, Quilt — detail, "Indian Crafts." Made by Sigrid Hedburg.

example, the spring of the pogo stick, features of the face, and the thread in the machine were all too linear to cut and appliqué, so embroidery was used instead.

Work all sections in a similar way. In a jigsaw puzzle construction, some shapes, like the fishbowl, may overlap two sections. In this situation, finish appliquéing the details after all the sections have been joined, either by machine or hand. As you finish your design, be flexible. Don't be afraid to change ideas as you go along. In this example, an umbrella, towel, and extra waves were added to soften the large, light area of the sand. Calico wildflowers now bloom around the picnic table. They were not part of the original design. Even the placement of the cyclist was shifted. Remember you, not the original pattern, are the boss.

Some Ideas About Fabrics and Sewing Notions

Fabric choices for your design can add personality to your piece. If you want smooth, neat hems, pick finely woven cotton or cotton-blend material.

However, a rough cloth like burlap can add a textural element that emphasizes the fun and informality of a subject.

Trims like rickrack can imitate architectural detailing.

Calicos can give life to hills and trees.

73

Colonial America — detail, "Betsey Ross and George Washington." Made by Hermione Cummings. Made in the New York City Bicentennial Urban Quilt Program. *Courtesy Jack Lipkins, photographer.*

Colonial America — detail, "Kitchen Interior." Made by Sachiko Uetake. Made in the New York City Bicentennial Urban Quilt Program. *Courtesy Jack Lipkins, photographer.*

Colonial America – detail, "Auction Day." Made by Eunice Samuels. Made in the New York City Bicentennial Urban Quilt Program. *Courtesy Jack Lipkins, photographer.*

Nautical Quilt – detail, "Fisherman with Netting" instructors, Celine Mahler and Anita Schlachter. Made in the New York City Bicentennial Urban Quilt Program. *Courtesy Jack Lipkins, photographer.*

Montana Quilt. Made by the Gallatin Chapter of the
National Women's Political Caucus. Sara Noel, coordinator.
90" x 85".

A particular print, like the one found for the bleak hills in an ice-fishing scene, can be used for a repeat pattern (p. 72).

Metallic fabric can simulate shiny objects, like glass (p. 73).

One designer even knitted a sweater to create the right texture for her appliqué (p. 73).

Actual beads, similar to those used by Indians, decorate the moccasin and pouch in a square depicting Iroquois artifacts (p. 73).

A Colonial maiden wears delicate laces. Notice also how the flag fabric actually drapes (p. 74).

In the same way, notice how the folds of green gauze clothe the Statue of Liberty (p. 73).

Even the tiniest details are appliquéd in a Colonial kitchen scene (p. 74). The finishing touch of this design is a small, metallic chain (p. 75).

Real netting helps to tell the fisherman's story (p. 75).

A final example illustrates other three-dimensional effects. The pheasant's tail is free-hanging. It flaps. The covered-wagon cover draws up, and some of Old Faithful's spray falls freely (p. 76).

Take a cue from these original pieces and let your imagination guide you in creating your own fanciful appliqué.

6 *The Art of Embroidery*

Embroidery, the art of stitching designs with colorful thread, follows a tradition over three-thousand years old. The early cultural histories of China, Egypt, Persia, Byzantium, and Peru all document textiles decorated with tiny stitches. In Europe, the art of embroidery reached its peak in seventeenth-century England. The work of Mary Queen of Scots exemplifies typical needlework of that era.

Embroidery Used to Create Line

Early American settlers brought the skills of embroidery with them to the New World. In an example dated 1740, all-over designs of scrolls and vines decorate a homespun linen coverlet. The various stitches of colored thread add a linear embellishment to this otherwise plain fabric.

Pictures drawn in outline stitches also have a linear quality. A child's spread from the early twentieth century displays coloring-booklike images. Made about the same time, a similar spread from Rome, Ohio, portrays local buildings.

Recently, embroidery outlines have served as map borders in quilts made in Schoharie County, New York, and Williamstown, Massachusetts.

Like the Williamstown quilters, the creators of the *Beaver, Pennsylvania,* and *Maryland Bicentennial* quilts write printed letter forms in thread, while Kay Olivia employs the flowing, linear

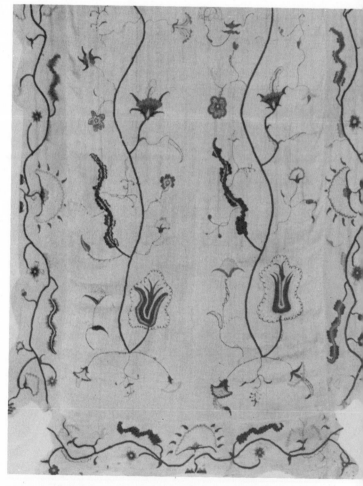

Linen bed cover embroidered in wool, Massachusetts, c. 1740. 87" x 72". *Courtesy Collections of The Greenfield Village and the Henry Ford Museum, Dearborn, Michigan.*

Child's picture quilt. Made by Emma Hartman, c. 1915. 66" x 57".

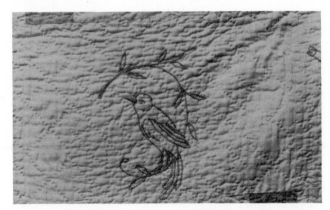

Child's picture quilt — detail. Made by Emma Hartman, c. 1915. 66" x 57".

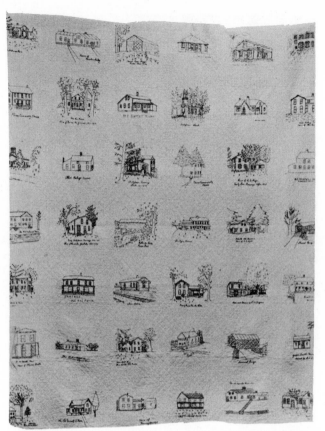

Rome, Ohio, Quilt. Made by the Ladies Benevolent Society of the Presbyterian Church, 1923.

Rome, Ohio, Quilt — detail.

quality of embroidered script to write explanations of details on her *The Revolution on Long Island* quilt.

Embroidery Used to Create Areas of Color

The color-filled arabesque shapes of a coverlet detail illustrate a completely different tradition of embroidery. Long, adjacent floats of threads color entire areas. The sheen of satin covers a whole scene in the *Santa Margarita School Quilt* from San Rafael, California. Similarly, in the "Mallard

Schoharie County, New York, Quilt. Sponsored by the Schoharie Colonial Heritage Association. Laura Kane, instructor. 100" x 80".

Bicentennial Quilt — detail. Made by the Women's Fellowship of the First Congregational Church of Williamstown, Massachusetts.

Maryland Quilt — detail.

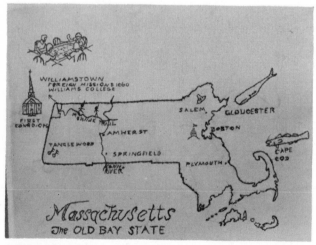

Bicentennial Quilt — detail. Made by the Women's Fellowship of the First Congregational Church of Williamstown, Massachusetts.

The Revolution on Long Island — detail. Made by Kay Olivia.

80

Beaver, Pennsylvania, Quilt – detail. Dolores Barclay, leader; Sarah Foster, instructor.

The Revolution on Long Island – detail. Made by Kay Olivia.

The Revolution on Long Island – detail. Made by Kay Olivia.

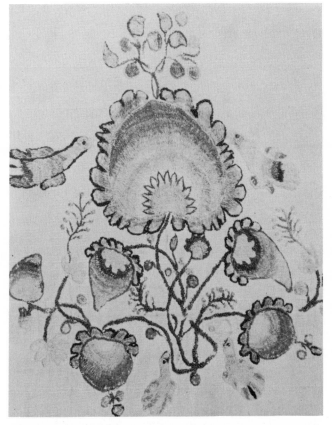

Quilt made by Keturah Young, Aquebogue, Long Island, New York, 1806. 93½" x 74". *Courtesy The Daughters of the American Revolution Museum, Gift of Mrs. Marjory Young Tyte.*

Santa Margarita School Quilt — detail. San Rafael, California.

Montana Critters — detail, "Mallard Drake." Made by Susan Wallace. *Courtesy Nancy Tobie.*

Drake" from Susan Wallace's *Montana Critters* quilt, the satiny stitches resemble the duck's glistening feathers.

Embroidery Used to Create Pattern

Women from the Pecos Valley in New Mexico add pattern stitches to linear and satin embroidery. It is not unusual for pattern stitches to dominate the visual interest of a piece. An early nineteenth-century example contains flat, cross, outline, satin, and buttonhole stitches — all of which form separate little patterns. Mary Guderjohn picks only one — the running stitch to put pattern into her rendering of "The University of Washington Football Stadium in the Rain."

Embroidery patterns not only add detail, but also can outline appliqué as illustrated in a mid-nineteenth-century coverlet made in Kentucky, and a contemporary example from the *Douglas County, Kansas, Quilt,* stitched by Louise Townsend.

The needleworker of the late 1800s often accepted the challenge to join each patch of a crazy quilt with a different embroidery pattern. The hours spent on these richly colored quilts were well spent, for the network of imaginative stitches is exquisite.

Several contemporary quilts display equal

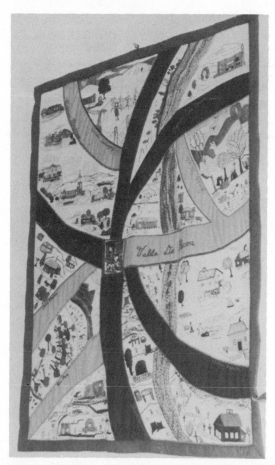

La Vida en el Valle de Pecos (Life in Pecos Valley). **Carmen Orrego-Salos, instructor; Helen Thompson, coordinator. 108" x 90".** *Courtesy International Folk Art Foundation collections in the Museum of International Folk Art, a division of the Museum of New Mexico, Santa Fe, New Mexico.*

82

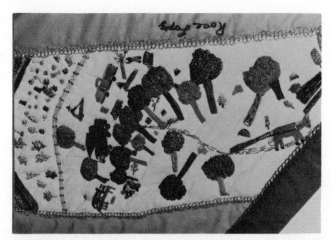

La Vida en el Valle de Pecos – detail.

La Vida en el Valle de Pecos – detail.

La Vida en el Valle de Pecos – detail.

La Vida en el Valle de Pecos – detail.

imagination and craftsmanship. Catherine Paul employs both the scroll-like line of our earliest example, and pattern possibilities in her modern-day *Impressions of Northern California.*

Elaine Yingling sews with one or two strands of

Quilt, 1810-1840. 74" x 61". *Courtesy The Henry Francis du Pont Winterthur Museum.*

Around Puget Sound — detail, "University of Washington Football Stadium in the Rain." Made by Mary Guderjohn.

Appliqué coverlet — detail. Made by Mrs. Benjamin Skene, 1866, in Louisville, Kentucky. *Index of American Design Photograph courtesy The National Gallery of Art, Washington, D.C.*

Douglas County, Kansas, Quilt — detail. Walkins Community Museum, Lawrence, Kansas. Made by Louise O. Townsend.

Appliqué coverlet. Made by Mrs. Benjamin Skene, 1866, in Louisville, Kentucky. *Index of American Design Photograph courtesy The National Gallery of Art, Washington, D.C.*

Crazy Quilt. Courtesy The Clinton County Historical Association Museum, Clinton County, New York.

Crazy Quilt — detail. Courtesy The Clinton County Historical Association Museum, Clinton County, New York.

Impressions of Northern California. **Made by Catherine Paul.** *Courtesy Chester Paul and Michael Corbit, photographers.*

cotton embroidery floss when she intricately pictures such scenes as a row of soldiers with their guns in a square showing the battle of Plattsburgh. For the bolder lines like the boat rigging and architectural detailing, she threads more strands through her needle. With needle and thread, she has created line, shape and pattern (p. 88).

Another example of stitchery in fine thread comes from Hawaii. Women at the Richard's Street Branch YWCA in Honolulu copied pictures drawn by Mary Leineweber. Under the direction of Marge Chatterley, their instructor, twelve women in an advanced stitchery group sewed with black lingerie thread, mercerized cotton/polyester, and embroidery cotton of various plies, to stitch their intricate, etchinglike renderings (p. 88).

How to Embroider

The preceding examples should encourage you to try your hand at the craft of embroidery. Books on this subject abound. The amount of information and possibilities are endless. However, the following seven illustrated stitches will furnish you with a vocabulary with which you can describe many scenes and their details. After you accomplish these stitches on your first projects, you may want to add to your battery of stitches by following the diagrams and instructions found in one of the many other books on the subject.

1. Blanket Stitch

The blanket stitch (buttonhole stitch) is especially useful for covering a turned-under edge. Work from left to right. Start with the knot on the underside of your work and come up with the needle at the edge of the fabric. Now pierce the appliquéd fabric about one quarter inch from the edge. Come up with the needle at the edge of the lower fabric. Hold the loop of thread with your left thumb. Pull the needle through and over the loop, in a straight line toward you, so that the stitch holds the thread along the edge of the appliquéd fabric.

2. Chain Stitch

Start with the knot on the underside of your work. Bring the needle up to the beginning of your outline. Hold the thread down with your thumb, pass the needle from right to left, under the fabric, then over the held-down thread. Pull the needle

Impressions of Northern California – detail. Made by Catherine Paul. *Courtesy Chester Paul and Michael Corbit, photographers.*

and thread to the left and hold taut, so that the stitch will remain a small loop. Insert the needle again near the base of the new stitch and create the next thread link in the chain.

3. Lazy Daisy

The lazy daisy is a variation of the chain stitch. Come up with the needle at the center of the daisy and make one loop as you did in the chain stitch. After a loop is made, poke the needle back through the fabric very near to the tip of the daisy petal, where the needle has just surfaced. Direct the needle back toward the center of the daisy and come up through the fabric. Make a new petal by rotating the fabric a little to your right.

4. Satin Stitch

This is good for filling in small areas with color. Bring the needle up at one edge of the shape to be covered. Insert the needle at the other edge and turn the needle toward the first edge. Push the

Impressions of Northern California – detail. Made by Catherine Paul. *Courtesy Chester Paul and Michael Corbit, photographers.*

Clinton County, New York, Quilt — detail, "Battle of Plattsburgh." Made by Elaine Yingling.

Hawaii — detail, "Aloha Tower." Made by Marge Chatterley.

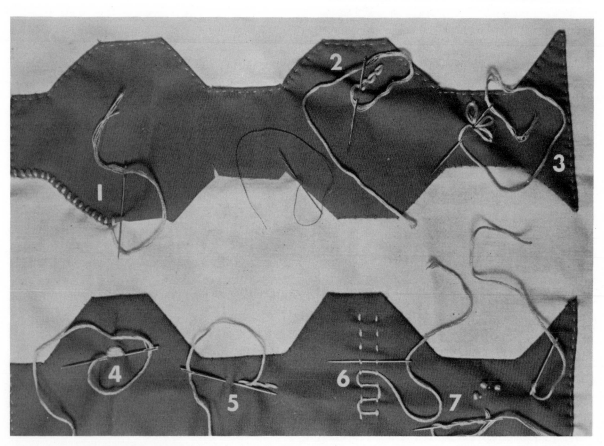

Seven Embroidery Stitches sampler.

needle under the fabric and up through it. You circle the fabric with the thread rotating above, then beneath the fabric. Make the second stitch the same way, very close to the first stitch, so that the fabric is well covered by the thread. Do not make satin stitches too long or they will be loose. To fill large areas with color, fill many small sections with satin stitches.

5. Outline Stitch (Stem or Crewel Stitch)

Reversed with the long floats underneath the fabric, this is called the back stitch. Turn the photograph upside down to follow these directions. Work from left to right. With the knot underneath, bring the needle up at the beginning of the line. Keep the needle always pointing to the left. Pull the thread over the fabric, to the right, a full stitch. Push the needle in and out of the fabric a half stitch to the left. Keep the thread below the needle. Repeat the stitch.

6. Serpentine Stitch

Sew two parallel rows of running stitches. With a third thread, lace back and forth between the parallel stitches.

7. French Knot

With the knot underneath, bring the needle up to the place where you want the French knot to be. Hold the thread about one and one-half inches from the source. Working from the eye of the needle toward the point, wind the thread one to three times around the needle. The number of times you wind depends upon the delicacy you wish. Hold the thread firmly. Insert the needle near the knot, but not into the same hole. Slide the knot down to the surface of the fabric. Pull the needle to the under side. The thread will go through the center of the knot, and will hold the twists in place.

7 Quilting

A Short History

Like the textile arts, appliqué, and embroidery, quilting also boasts a long history. Museums document that both the ancient Egyptians and the Chinese knew the technique. Evidences of quilting also abound in illustrations from medieval and Renaissance Europe. Notice the robe's quilted border in this one example of a Dürer pen drawing.

With other textile skills, Colonists brought the idea of quilting with them to their new home in America. A perfection of the craft developed.

Quilting specifically refers to the stitching that holds a top fabric, a filling material, and a bottom cloth together. Because of the air pockets that result, the product is both light in weight and a good insulation against the cold. Moveover, the puckered material between the paths of tiny stitches offers a surface for decoration. As the art of quilting progressed, needlewomen accentuated the three-dimensional or bas-relief character of the raised areas, by pushing extra filling through the bottom cloth and into the air pockets — a technique known as trapunto.

A fantastic example, made in 1856, represents a fair ground near Russellville, Kentucky. This detail shows the judging ring with parading horses, buggies, cows, men, sheep, and pigs. Reportedly there are 150 stitches per square inch of quilt. Note that the design arises simply from the quilting stitches. No embroidery or appliqué appears.

Two examples made by professional craftswomen illustrate a contemporary approach to this tradition. The pieces should inspire other craftsmen to work on a solid-colored fabric in a similar way.

Added to appliqué and embroidery, quilting can also help complete a picture. In this square showing "The Battle of Valcour, 1776," the running stitches cover the water in wavelike paths, and the hills in treelike configurations. As a result the picture is further developed and the backside of the square has a design of its own.

In this close-up photograph of the *Georgia Bicentennial Quilt,* the Old Campbell County Quilting Society represented the bicentennial symbol in quilting. Typical of many other quilts, the basic shapes and the border are similarly outlined with small stitches.

How to Quilt

In the past, quilts contained such oddments as paper, fleece, linen tow, goose down, blankets, or flannel sheets for insulation. Now filling can be of cotton, dacron, kapok, or polyester batting, sold for this purpose. The methods of quilting vary, but not any one is difficult. Perhaps the easiest way is working on small squares, the way the Brooklyn quilters are (p. 95).

First cut the batting and the backing the same size as the square. Next baste all three layers together so that they will not slip when you are working. Quilt your square with small running stitches. Try to hide all the knots. You can often start your first stitch under a piece of appliqué or

90

Holy Trinity by Albrecht Durer, Germany 1515. Pen drawing. *Courtesy Museum of Fine Arts, Boston.*

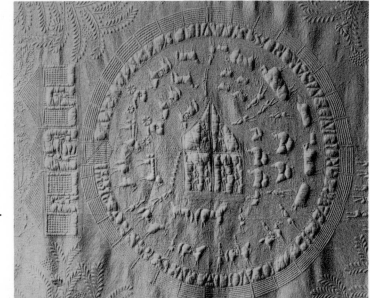

Fairground — detail. Made by Virginia Ivey in 1856. *Courtesy The Smithsonian Institution.*

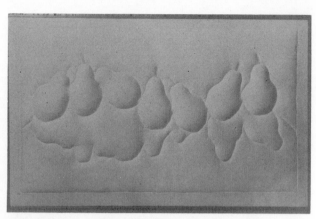

Pears. Made by Kathee O'Brien.

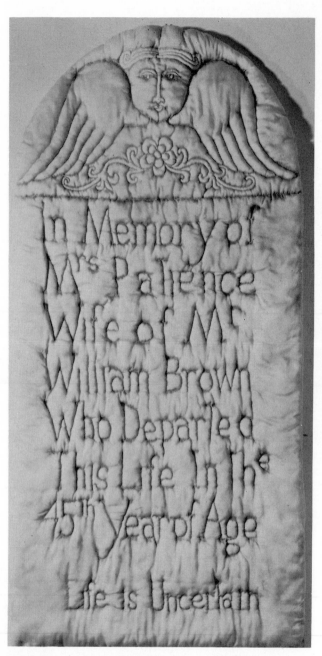

Clinton County, New York, Quilt — detail, "Battle of Valcour, 1776." Made by Nina Holland.

Life Is Uncertain. Made by Elsa Brown. Single-bed size.

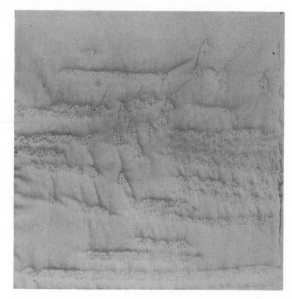

Clinton County, New York, Quilt — detail, "Battle of Valcour, 1776." Reverse side.

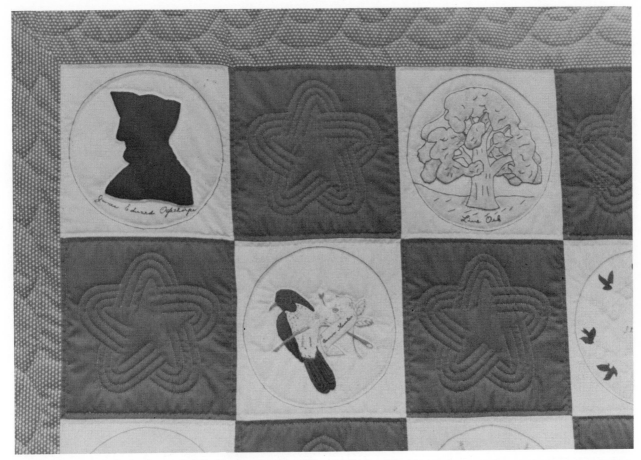

Georgia Bicentennial Quilt — detail. Made by the Old Campbell Quilting Society, Fairburn, Georgia.

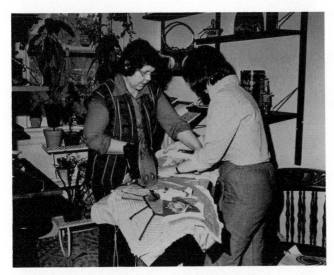

Women working on the *Made in Brooklyn* quilt.

on the outside border where it will not show. Or you can gently pull on your first stitch so that the knot is drawn into the inside of the layered cloth. When two squares are completed, with wrong sides together, sew a one-half inch seam to join the two squares. Iron the seam open. Turn under a one-quarter inch hem on either side of a two-inch-wide band. Quilt the band in place. The quilting stitches should penetrate the band, the top, the stuffing, and the backing (Figs. C and D).

If a band would cover too much of your design, try this alternative method. With a one-quarter inch hem, stitch a two inch band of backing material to the wrong side of the three-layered square. Cut a one and one-half inch-wide strip of batting. With a one-quarter inch hem, sew two inches of the border color to the right side of one square. Quilt through all layers. Pull the border fabric across the backing and stuffing. Turn a one-quarter inch hem and quilt the panel to the other square. When you have several rows of squares, you can join them with longer bands, as shown (Fig. D).

Three fabrics of a square stacked to show the different textures.

Figure B

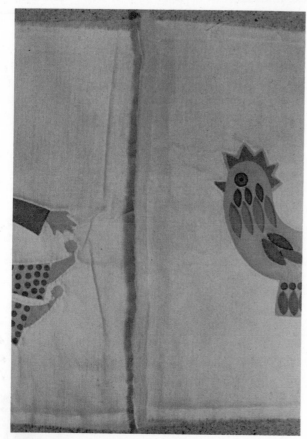

Figure C

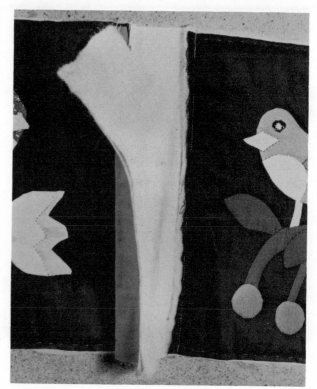

Figure D

Made in Brooklyn quilt in progress.

Oberlin, Ohio, quilters setting up the quilting frame. Inside edges of boards are covered with fabric. *Courtesy Jean Tufts, photographer.*

Molly Upton working on *Watchtower* on a ready-made quilt frame.

Oberlin, Ohio, quilters starting to quilt. *Courtesy Jean Tufts, photographer.*

For block or other style quilts, the quilting frame offers another method of joining all layers of fabric together. After the quilt top is completed, cut batting and backing material to the same size. If you don't have a ready-made quilting frame, put together one of your own. Cut four boards (two by four inch lumber is recommended) twelve inches longer than your quilt top. Cover by tacking down three sides of one edge on each board, with a tightly woven fabric. Hold the corners of the frame together with C clamps. Baste the stretched three layers of quilting materials to the cloth covering the frame edges. Start from the outside edges and baste through the sandwich of fabrics. As you finish basting the outside edges, you can roll the quilt on two of the parallel boards and clamp them again in place.

Another way of securing the frame corners is shown by the Vermont quilters, who had slits drilled in two of their boards. A wing-nut bolt slides along the slit and can be tightened at any one point.

After basting the piece, you can start the actual quilting either from the center working out, or from one side of the quilt to the opposite side. For a small piece, Lilian Bell uses the frame for basting only, and does the quilting on her lap. Here Lilian removes staples, which she prefers to stitches, for stretching the quilt to the frame. Notice how her quilt overlaps the corners of the frame. The paper protects the cloth from possible damage by the C clamps.

Another device that is helpful for lap work is a large hoop that stretches and holds the fabric over a smaller hoop.

A popular way to handle the border is also shown. To do this, cut the backing eight and one-half inches larger, and the batting four inches larger than the top fabric. Center the layers. Cut a two inch diagonal off of each corner. Turn in a

The Buffalo Bill appliquéd quilt — detail. Pennsylvania, c. 1880. From the Collections of the Henry Ford Museum, Dearborn, Michigan.

From the *Tisbury Town Quilt* — detail, "Steamship."

Birmingham Bloomfield Art Association Quilt, Michigan.

From *Oberlin, Ohio, Quilt* – detail, "Oberlin Bicyclers." Made by Audrey Pearson. *Courtesy Jean Tufts, photographer.*

Members of the Woman's Fellowship of the First Congregational Church of Williamstown, Massachusetts, quilt on frame with C clamps holding the corners of the frame.

Lilian Bell pulls out staples after she has basted her quilt fabrics together.

Vermont women working on quilt with slits and wing nut bolt. *Courtesy Ellen Foscue-Johnson, photographer.*

Embroidery hoop.

Valparaiso, Indiana, Quilt showing basting threads and quilting stitches.

Oberlin, Ohio, quilters binding the edge of their quilt. *Courtesy Jean Tufts, photographer.*

Ozaukee County, Wisconsin, Quilt in progress. Sewer holds her needle at right angles to the work.

Lake Fairlee, Vermont, Quilt in progress.

Nanhant, Massachusetts, quilters feeling underneath the quilt for the next place to stitch.

one-quarter inch hem. Turn under the excess fabric to miter the corners. Baste, then sew the border in place.

Another solution for edges is to bind them with a strip of fabric that matches the quilt's top.

The detail from the *Lake Fairlee, Vermont, Quilt* shows basting threads and quilting in progress. The quilting follows the appliqué outlines, a pictorial pattern, and the border motif. Because quilting stitches should be close together, the quilter, when working on a frame, pokes her needle directly down and at right angles to the top. With her other hand she first grasps the needle, then feels with her fingers where the next stitch should go, and finally shoots the needle up from beneath. Modern quilters can appreciate stories about fine needleworkers not winning a fair prize because of a small bloodstain from a pricked finger.

Hanging and Care of Quilts

If your quilt is to be hung, you will want to devise an arrangement to keep the weight stress evenly distributed. You may decide to sew loops and attach them to the border fabric at frequent intervals. Or you can simply add curtain rings across the top. Another idea is to sew, traversing the top of the back, a long, two inch sleeve that can hold a rod.

If you want to permanently affix the hanging to a wall you can attach grommets and bolt the quilt to the wall through the grommet holes. Or epoxy one side of velcro strips to a wall, and sew the matching side to the quilt top. Press the quilt in place.

Dust can harm your fabric, so vacuum it occasionally to help preserve it. A spray protector can also help, but eventually your piece may need to be hand-washed or dry-cleaned, so keep a record of the materials you have used and the recommended care of each fiber type.

Also, bright light will fade almost any dye, so keep your piece out of direct light as well as you can.

We now appreciate those old quilts well preserved for our enjoyment. For the same reason, you will want your quilt to last for many decades.

8 *Other Techniques*

Textile artists are now reaching beyond traditional materials and methods to create their quilts. The horse from the *Brookline Heights Center Quilt* illustrates how a bold texture can add a new dimension to an otherwise plain drawing. The *Made in Brooklyn* quilt not only incorporates rough fibers, but also metal work, leaded glass, shells, buttons, stuffed figures, and small toys. Besides appliqué and embroidery, these artists employed needlepoint, bargello, hooking, crocheting, and photography to fashion their design.

For the complex shapes of cartoonlike figures, Michiko Sato swung away from the usual woven cloth and chose felt instead, which does not need hemming. The images, from her son's doodles also reflect a new idea for subject matter.

The "Indian Salmon" design illustrates another less usual technique — reverse appliqué. The design comes from tiny fabrics pieced from underneath, rather than layered on top of one another. Instead of covering the large fabric pieces with a smaller one to the color change, holes are cut into the largest fabric. The smaller shape is filled in from behind. It is then cut, and an even smaller piece is set in for another color change.

Stuffed forms riding on a quilt illustrate the ultimate in three-dimensional design. Imagine sleeping under this miniature village with the church steeple perched on the end of your toe and the fields lying across your stomach. It is Robert Louis Stevenson's fantasy come true (p. 102).

THE LAND OF COUNTERPANE

When I was sick and lay a-bed,
I had two pillows at my head,
And all my toys beside me lay
To keep me happy all the day.

And sometimes for an hour or so
I watched my leaden soldiers go,
With different uniforms and drills,
Amoung the bed-clothes, through the hills;

And sometimes sent my ships in fleets
All up and down among the sheets;
Or brought my trees and houses out,
And planted cities all about.

I was the giant great and still
That sits upon the pillow-hill,
And sees before him, dale and plain,
The pleasant land of counterpane.

Brookline Heights Center Quilt – detail.

100

Made in Brooklyn. Maddie Appel and Linda Blyer, instructors. Made in the New York City Bicentennial Urban Quilt Program. *Courtesy Jack Lipkins, photographer.*

Kenzo's Super Heroes. Made by Michiko Sato. 7' x 6'.

Vermont Village — detail. Made by Gail Kiesler. *Courtesy Erik Borg, photographer.*

Around Puget Sound — detail, "Indian Salmon." Made by Cindy Katzka. *Courtesy Cathi Gunderson, photographer.*

Vermont Village. Made by Gail Kiesler. 108" x 90". *Courtesy Erik Borg, photographer.*

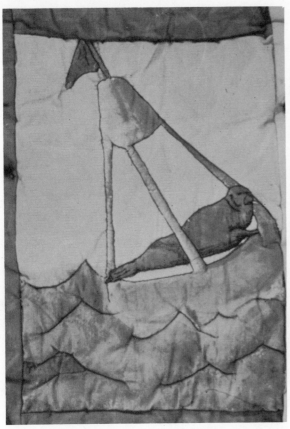

Autumn Equinox. Made by Lilian Bell.

Sailboat on San Francisco Bay — detail, "Seal on a Buoy."
Made by Merrylee Smith.

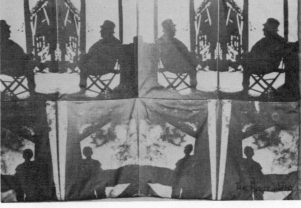

The American Wing II — detail. Made by Tafi Brown.

Quilted batik bedspread — detail. Made by Stephen and
Teresa Blumrich.

The Growing Keiters. Made by Joan Keiter. 96" x 74".

The Growing Keiters — detail. Made by Joan Keiter.

Reiche School Bicentennial Quilt. Made by Julianne Kilmartin's fourth-, fifth-, and sixth-grade art students, Portland, Maine. 7½' x 5½'.

Silk screening in process for the Green Bay, Wisconsin, quilt.

Quilting a square for the *Green Bay, Wisconsin, Quilt.*

105

Green Bay, Wisconsin, Quilt. 108" x 75".

Besides appliqué, quilters can create images by directly coloring and dyeing fabric, as the work of the following four professional artists show. Merrylee Smith paints a dye onto her piece. This detail of a seal on a buoy is one chapter in her picture story of a sailboat on San Francisco Bay.

Stephen Blumrich, an experienced craftsman, batiked (dyed with a wax resist on the fabric) fine detailed squares and rectangles. His wife, Teresa, tailored the pieces into the extraordinary quilt.

Lilian Bell combined stitchery, appliqué, tie-dyeing, spray dyeing, and direct dyeing design elements for her surrealistic *Autumn Equinox*. The fiber-reactive dyes that these artists use come in bright colors, penetrate the fabric, and resist fading. They are now available from a number of suppliers.

Ballpoint embroidery markers and fiber crayons offer alternative ways to paint color onto fabric.

Innovative quilters have also adopted photographic images for their designs. In a series of five quilts, Tafi Brown has recorded the initial construction of a home built for her parents by her brothers. She used the cyanotype process. First, she coated the light-sensitive solution on one-hundred percent cotton. Onto this she made a contact print with a codalith negative. A blue image, appropriately reminiscent of blue prints, resulted. She played upon reverse images to devise her pattern.

Joan Keiter compiled another family-theme quilt from cyanotype prints made from photographs recording the life of the Keiter family. Album quilts of the 1840s have evolved into photo album quilts of the 1970s.

Several quilt groups have silk-screened their depictions. In this more familiar technique, the printer can make many copies of one image. The quilter can repeat several copies of different designs in a spread, or use a single printed fabric for a framed picture, pillow cover, tray liner, or placemat. The Green Bay Wisconsin members of the Antiquarian Society used the photo silk-screen process and have found that the sale of small items is a good money-maker.

It is evident that the growth of interest in quilting is not only profuse but also varied in technique and style.

9 *A Tour of Local Heritage Quilts*

Many quilts with a historical theme developed as a result of the 1976 United States bicentennial. Intended as banners rather than as functional bedspreads, they now proudly hang in communities all over the country. The following pages will guide you on a tour of these quilts. As you thread your way along this path, you will see both the similarities and the differences among the local heritages portrayed by their residents — those who can best testify to the character of their hometowns. The quilts offer views of America through the eyes of many citizens.

On many quilts, buildings erected in the eighteenth and nineteenth centuries stand, the symbols of life and events that have passed through them. The silhouettes, as they appear on each quilt, remind the citizenery of past generations, of public ceremonies, and of particular historic dramas. The architecture, with its fine detailing, is reminiscent of the days when the price of labor and materials allowed for individual craftsmanship and the unique personality of each building that resulted.

Patchwork of fields, roads, and land reoccurs as a pictorial theme in many of these quilts. The open spaces foil the inhabited buildings on the landscape.

People appear here as heroes of a local story, there simply as a neighbor at a daily task.

The distinction between landscapes and wildlife helps set apart one local quilt from another. Landmarks of human conflict in war and legend give each quilt a special significance. It is these as well as the aesthetic differences which make each quilt a special folk-art work, worthy of our study.

Gorham, Maine, Quilt — detail showing Captain John Phinney and son, both early settlers, cutting timber for their first cabin.

107

Gorham, Maine, Quilt. Made under the leadership of Tania Hannon. Presently displayed at Gorham Town Hall.

Rockport, Maine, Quilt. Made under the leadership of Kitty Jenkins. 90" x 72". *Courtesy Barnes Photo.*

Rockport, Maine, Quilt – detail.

Historic Boscawen, New Hampshire, Quilt. Evelyn Bassett, leader. 81" x 95".

Lyme Town, New Hampshire, Quilt — detail, "Edgell Bridge." Made by Ervill Franklin.

Hopkinton, New Hampshire, Quilt. Doris Luneau, leader. 94" x 80".

Lyme Town, New Hampshire, Quilt — detail, "Town Meeting." Made by Marti Warren.

Lyme Town, New Hampshire, Quilt — detail, "Fair." Made by Pamela Wilcox.

Lyme Town, New Hampshire, Quilt — top. Section two.
7' x 7'.

Lyme Town, *New Hampshire, Quilt* – top. Section one.
7' x 7'.

Quilt designed by Ed Larson, Kansas City, Missouri.

Birmingham Bloomfield Art Association Quilt – detail.
Made by Jim Balmer.

Worcester, Massachusetts, Quilt — detail. Made by the students at Burncoat Junior High.

Family Quilt. 40" x 36". Made by Nina Holland.

Orwell, Vermont, Landmarks Quilt. Cecelia Barnes, leader.
84" x 84".

Middlebury, Vermont, Quilt. Sponsored by the Congregational Church Women's Fellowship. 104" x 85".

New Canaan, Connecticut, Quilt. Designed by Ann Price. 88" x 75". Displayed at New Canaan Historical Society.

Wilton, Connecticut, Quilt — detail shows house owned by the Wilton Historical Society and entrance to local cemetery.

Tisbury Town Quilt, Martha's Vineyard, Massachusetts. Shark pictured not from the landscape, but symbol of the movie *Jaws*, so popular in 1975. 6½' x 9½'.

Wilton, Connecticut, Quilt. Alice Moir, chairperson. Owned by the Wilton Historical Society. 8½' x 11'.

Nahant Historical Society Quilt, Nahant, Massachusetts. Mary Conlin, coordinator. Quilt displayed at the Nahant Public Library. 94" x 94".

Brookline Arts Center Quilt, Brookline, Massachusetts. Fred O'Connell, coordinator. 94" x 76".

Historical Warmth. Made at Harrington School, Lexington, Massachusetts by Constance Arlander's third- and fourth-grade students.

Montclair, New Jersey, Quilt — detail, "Israel Crane House," built in 1796.

Montclair, New Jersey, Quilt. 108" x 96". Sponsored by
the Montclair Crafters Guild.

Lavallette's Historical Towne, Lavallette, New Jersey. Designed by Carol Ham. 108" x 72".

The Alliance Unitarian Church Bicentennial Quilt, Montclair, New Jersey — detail.

Cinnaminson, New Jersey, Quilt. 54" x 64".

Onondaga County, New York, Quilt — detail, "Jerry Rescue, An Underground Railroad Story." Made by Mary Ann Laffredo and Mary Helen Foster.

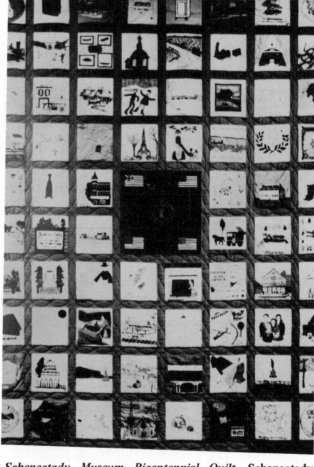

Schenectady Museum Bicentennial Quilt, Schenectady, New York. 104" x 84".

Clinton County, New York, Quilt. 84" x 66". Joyce Grover and Elaine Yingling, leaders. Owned by Clinton County Historical Society.

Clinton County, New York, Quilt. 84" x 66". Joyce Grover and Elaine Yingling, leaders. Owned by Clinton County Historical Society.

Saugerties, New York, Quilt. 105" x 85". Marie Genthner, organizer.

North Tarrytown, New York, Quilt. 82" x 82". Displayed in village hall of North Tarrytown.

The Revolution on Long Island. Made by Kay Olivia. 102" x 78".

Beaver Area Landmarks, Beaver, Pennsylvania. Dolares Barclay, leader; Sarah Foster, instructor. 84" x 72". *Courtesy John H. Ripper, photographer.*

New York, New York: Still a Wonderful Town. Sponsored by the New York State Board of Education, Department of Art and Home Economics. Created by teachers in an in-service workshop. Celine Mahler, instructor. Made in the New York City Bicentennial Urban Quilt Program. *Courtesy Jack Lipkins, photographer.*

Beaver Area Landmarks, Beaver, Pennsylvania — detail, "Fort McIntosh," which played a significant role in prerevolutionary and revolutionary war.

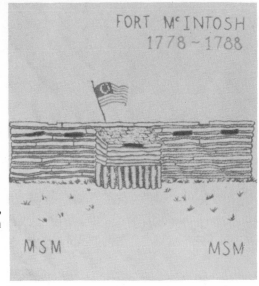

Anne Arundel County Landmark Quilt, Maryland. Double-bed size. *Courtesy M.E. Warren, photographer.*

Annapolis, Maryland, Quilt. Double-bed size.

Maryland Quilt – detail, "Wye Oak."

Maryland Quilt. Made by members of the Holy Cross Lutheran Church of Greenbelt, Maryland. 108" x 90".

Loudoun County, Virginia, Quilt. Made by the Loudoun Extension Homemakers Club. 100" x 68".

South Carolina Quilt. Mrs. Wayne Link, instructor. 6½' x 5½'. Pendleton District Historical Commission, owner.

Gwinnett County, Georgia, Quilt. Made by Lucile Baldwin and quilted by the Sweetwater Community Chapel Quilters. 9' x 7'.

Georgia Quilt. Made by the Old Campbell County Quilting Society, Fairburn, Georgia. Dot Barrett, leader. 68" x 68".

Mariemont, Ohio, Quilt – detail, "Town Crier." Made by Hope Kain. *Courtesy Rob Paris, photographer.*

Mariemont, Ohio, Quilt – detail, "Town Square at Christmas." Made by Roberta Bolling. *Courtesy Rob Paris, photographer.*

Mariemont, Ohio, Quilt – detail, "Community Church." Made by Carolyn Schwenkmeyer. *Courtesy Rob Paris, photographer.*

Mariemont, Ohio, Quilt. 110" x 95". Courtesy Rob Paris, photographer.

Oberlin, Ohio, Quilt. Ricky Clark, instructor. 100" x 74".
Courtesy Robert Stillwell, photographer.

Oberlin, Ohio, Quilt – detail, "Oberlin Bicyclers." Made by Audrey Pearson. *Courtesy Jean Tufts, photographer.*

Mahoning Valley, Youngstown, Ohio, Quilt – detail.

Cincinnati, Ohio, Quilt. 115" x 90". Made by Anderson Hills Adult Recreation Class. *Courtesy Cincinnati Art Museum.*

Mahoning Valley, Youngstown, Ohio, Quilt. 93" x 78".

Valparaiso, Indiana, Quilt. 88" x 88". Joan Dugen, chairperson.

Birmingham, Michigan, Quilt. Made by Birmingham Bloom-field Art Association. Rosemary Squires, coordinator; Jo Edwards, designer. Displayed at the Allen House.

Naperville, Yesterday and Today, Naperville, Illinois. Made by Art Guild of Naperville. 95" x 82".

Huntington Woods, Michigan, Quilt. Nancy Carlson, chairperson. 95½" x 64½". Displayed at City of Huntington Woods Library. *Courtesy Richard Clapp, photographer.*

Moultrie County, Illinois, Quilt – detail.

Moultrie County, Illinois, Quilt. Mary Oathout, leader. Made by Moultrie County Homemakers Extension Association.

Harvard, Illinois, Quilt. Designed by Barbara Andrew. Rosalyn Farmer, coordinator. 93" x 80".

Harvard, Illinois, National Quilt. Designed by Barbara Andrew. Rosalyn Farmer, coordinator.

Our American Heritage, Elgin, Nebraska. Made by Domestic Arts Club. 110" x 90".

Hastings, Nebraska, Quilt — detail.

Hastings, Nebraska, Quilt. Mary Laning, instructor. 96" x 80".

Early Lexington, Nebraska — detail, "Ira W. Olive House," built in 1892. Mr. Olive was a member of the Olive gang, who feuded with the settlers between the 1870s and 1880s.

Early Lexington, Nebraska — detail, "Cornland Hotel."

Early Lexington, Nebraska. 103" x 90".

Ames, Iowa, Quilt. Carolee Knutson and Charlotte Menzel, leaders. 111" x 94". *Courtesy Richard L. Knutson, photographer.*

Buildings in the National Register of Historic Buildings, Green Bay, Wisconsin. Made by De Pere Antiquarian Society. Amanda Cobb, leader. 75" x 108". Silk screened.

Brown County, Minnesota, Quilt. Joyce Aufderheide, coordinator. Owned by Brown County Historical Society Museum.

Brown County, Minnesota, Quilt – detail.

Douglas County, Kansas, Quilt – detail, "Barn." Made by Chris Edmonds.

Douglas County, Kansas, Quilt – detail, "Coal Creek Library," in Vinland, Kansas. Made by Jean Mitchell.

Douglas County, Kansas, Quilt – detail, "First Unitarian Church," in Lawrence, Kansas. Made by Thelma Helyar.

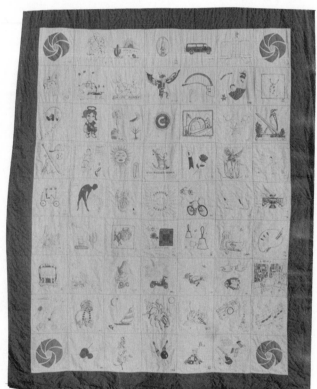

Sun City, Arizona, Quilt. Sponsored by Sun Bowl Plaza Merchants Association. 9'4" x 7'10".

Douglas County, Kansas, Quilt – detail, "Thacher House," in Lawrence, Kansas. Made by Pat Drewry.

Colorado Springs County, Colorado, quilt: *Pictorial History of Pikes Peak Region.* Silver Key Agency, sponsor. Mrs. Kenneth Keene and Mrs. William Fischer, chairpersons. 108" x 84". Owned by the Pioneer Museum, Colorado Springs, Colorado.

National Quilt. Made by parents and friends of children in Santa Margarita School, San Rafael, California. Sally Hauser, leader. 89" x 76".

Sonoma County, California, Quilt — detail. Made by Terra Newman.

Sonoma County, California, Quilt. Terra Newman, leader. 84" x 96".

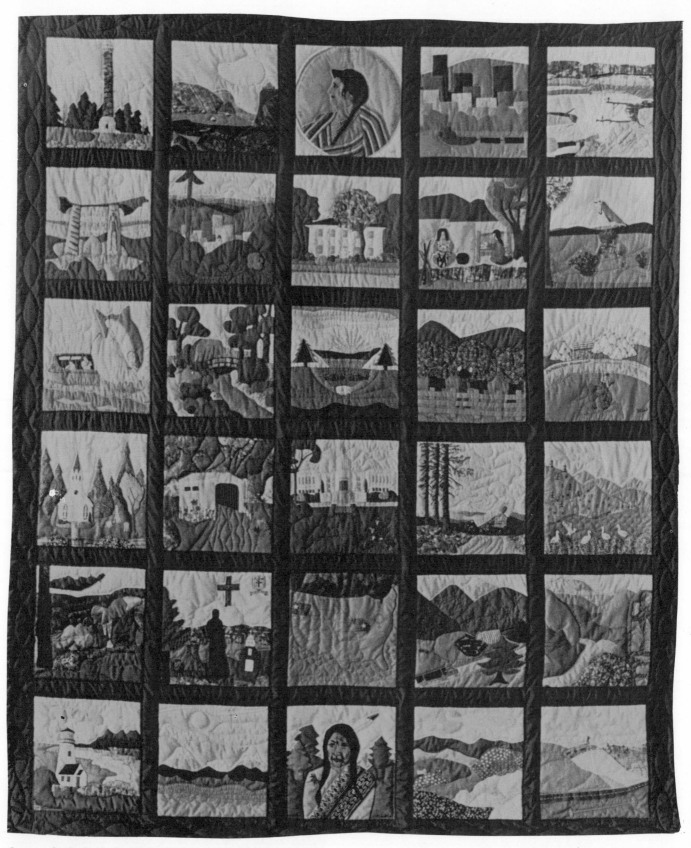

Oregon Quilt. DeLoris Stude, leader. 96" x 84". Owned by
the Oregon Historical Society.

Long Beach, California, Historical Quilt. Betty Olson and Robert Barrett, leaders. Sponsored by the Long Beach Recreation Department. 88" x 68".

Josephine County Historical Quilt – detail, "Football Field." Made by American Field Service. Nancy Murphy, leader.

Josephine County Historical Quilt – detail, "Almond Tree in Bloom." Made by American Field Service. Nancy Murphy, leader.

Columbia Gorge and Surrounding Country, Washington.
Made by Friends of the Library, White Salmon, Washington.

Around Puget Sound, Washington — detail, "Pike Place Market." Made by Kathleen Stang. *Courtesy Cathi Gunderson, photographer.*

Clark County, Washington, Historical Quilt. Sarah Lee, instructor. 94" x 84".

Around Puget Sound, Washington. Kathleen Stang, instructor. *Courtesy Cathi Gunderson, photographer.*

Around Puget Sound, Washington — detail, "Space Needle and Science Center Arches from the Seattle World's Fair." Made by Cathi Gunderson. *Courtesy, Cathi Gunderson, photographer.*

Hawaii quilt. Made by Richards Street Branch YWCA, Advanced Stitchery Class. Mary Leineweber, artist; Marge Chatterley, instructor; Yvonne Brown, coordinator. 102" x 90".

Books of Interest

Brown, Elsa. *Creative Quilting.* New York: Watson and Guptill Publications, 1975.

Lane, Rose Wilder. *Woman's Day Book of American Needlework.* New York: Simon and Schuster, 1963.

Laury, Jean Ray. *Quilts and Coverlets.* New York, Cincinnati, Toronto, London, Melbourne: Van Nostrand-Reinhold, 1970.

Meilach, Dona Z. *Batik and Tie-Dye.* New York: Crown Publishers, Inc., 1973.

Orlofsky, Patsy and Myron. *Quilts in America.* New York, St. Louis, San Francisco, Dusseldorf, London, Mexico, Sydney, Toronto: McGraw Hill Book Co., 1974.

Safford, Carleton l., and Bishop, Robert. *America's Quilts and Coverlets.* New York: Weathervane Books a division of Barre Publishing Co., Inc., by arrangement with E.P. Dutton & Co., Inc., 1974.

Index